Justine

Scattered

Acknowledgement is made to the Alfred Music Publishing for permission to
use lyrics from "It Had to Be You" by Gus Kahn
ISBN: 0-6156-5791-5
ISBN-13: 9780615657912

Scattered

Justine Hope Blau

2012

"Reading Scattered can be an almost wistful experience—you find yourself wishing for the lost New York landscape Justine Blau describes—but what grips you is what's timeless: her experience as a child subject to the whims of a bipolar mother who wanders from hotel to hotel. Blau shows us the love children feel for one another and the secret bonds they share. No one should be treated the way Blau was (it broke me down, reading this), but the childhood she describes is still rich with wonder. Her tone is honest and clear-eyed—and quite amazingly, filled more with more pity for others than for herself. You should read this."
Meakin Armstrong, fiction editor, *Guernica*

"In her fascinating story about a young girl set adrift and homeless when her family falls apart, Blau tells what it was like to grow up on the streets of New York haplessly towed around by her mentally ill mother. While her mother believes she is offering her daughter an extraordinary adventure, we see a young girl in an impossible situation: desperate for the stability of regular meals, a bed, and to be allowed to go to school most days, yet also fiercely loyal to a mother she loves. Blau's unblinking storytelling holds everyone accountable and yet allows for a place of forgiveness."
Maureen Ryan, co-producer of *Man on Wire* **and** *Project Nim*

"The writing is lively and appealing, and Blau clearly has a gift for storytelling."
David Hajdu, author *The Ten Cent Plague* **and** *Positively 4*th **Street**

For Asher and Grace

"I'll gladly pay you Tuesday for a hamburger today."

J. Wellington Wimpy (from *Popeye)*

Chapter 1.

The Glamour Girl in Queens

"Justine, who are you fighting?"

I was five years old, standing in the nursery school yard, punching the air with all my might, but the teacher's words pulled me back to reality. She watched me, concerned, perplexed, unsure of what to do. The kids on the jungle gym behind me were watching me too. I lowered my fists and walked inside, embarrassed.

The day before, my eyes were glued to my mother while she fought on the street with a large Greek woman. They struggled against each other, their arms overhead, hands gripping and pushing, two hefty lionesses in flowery dresses. Like me, the woman's daughter stood there, but instead of watching her mother, she glared at me.

"Ya stinking schmata rag!" my mother yelled, and shoved the other woman who lurched back.

I didn't exactly know what was going on, just that it wasn't good, somehow connected to the incident when my brother, Jake, had called the Greek woman's daughter fat. Now the mother had lunged at mine. Finally, they fell back, staring each other down until the other woman broke off, spat, grabbed her daughter and left.

"Did you see how I kept my mouth closed?" my mother asked. "She's a nut and it's a terrible thing to fight someone. But if you ever have to fight, protect your teeth by keeping your mouth closed."

Inside my nursery school, I needed to pee, but I wouldn't give in. The teacher, who had followed me in kept watch as I ran from chair to chair, clutching their backs in an effort to control the mounting pressure. Earlier that morning, when my mother dropped me off, I heard the teacher tell her that the nursery school bill was overdue.

Although the teacher gently encouraged me to go to the bathroom, it felt like a matter of pride to hold my pee in, even as I realized it was a losing battle. With a mixture of shame and relief, the hot, wet pee spread across my bottom and down one leg of my bright blue corduroy pants. Quietly, the teacher handed me a pair of dungarees and I put them on.

The four of us—my older brother, Leo, who was fourteen, Jake, eleven, my mother and I—were living in Astoria, Queens, in a sunny three-bedroom co-op apartment development. Trees and bushes clustered around benches between the 14-story buildings, framed by well-cared-for lawns. Playgrounds for little kids and asphalt courts where the older kids played half-court basketball, football and catch, punctuated the quiet community.

I had my own bedroom and on weekends Jake played house with me. We'd drape a blanket between a small table and chair in the living room, crawl underneath and play checkers or the card game War. At night I chanted to my brothers, "Tell me a story, sing me a song," and they would.

There was the story about the little man who climbed up the brick wall to our fifth-floor apartment and Leo gave him my nutted cream cheese sandwich on raisin bread that Mom had brought back from Chock full o'Nuts in Manhattan. I hadn't been able to finish my sandwich and left it in the fridge to have for breakfast, but in the morning it was gone. Leo explained what happened.

"In the middle of the night, a tiny old man climbed up to our window and knocked on it and said his wife was very hungry and could she have something to eat. So I gave him the cream cheese sandwich on date nut bread. I felt sorry for him."

I was delighted that he gave the sandwich to the little man. *I loved believing the story, and soon after, when I realized he'd made it up, I also loved knowing that he had concocted such a story.*

Some days when my brothers were at school—Leo at the Bronx High School of Science and Jake at PS 112—Mom would take me with her to Manhattan for the day where she'd shop or go to a lecture or other grown up things, and we'd come home at twilight on the elevated RR train. In hot weather, the train's slow-moving overhead fans were useless against the humidity, and the torn wicker seats stuck to the back of my legs and pulled at my skin when I got up. But I inhaled the aroma of freshly baked bread from the Silvercup factory near Queens Plaza and rested my cheek on Mom's plump upper arm. Her skin was cool and comforting.

One Sunday morning in June, nearby church bells woke me up. From my bedroom window I could see the big kids' playground where just one kid, a friend of Leo's, wearing a Jughead hat, squatted to play a game of *skully* with bottle caps on the ground.

I got out of bed and picked up my coonskin cap. My toy chest was filled with my older brothers' old costumes and toy guns, the red and white cowgirl outfit my father had bought for me, and lots of stuffed animals. I had plenty of dolls too, who sat in their doll carriage with its lavish pink ribbon.

I walked out to the living room and planted myself on the chartreuse vinyl couch, watching unnoticed as my mother puttered around the kitchen.

My mother had radiant skin, sparkling brown eyes, straight white teeth, a Grecian nose and lustrous black hair—a Jewish Jackie Kennedy she called herself. Except she was heftier, *zaftig*; if I put my arms around her, I could not completely encircle her girth, but she said men liked women that way. Her mother told her she didn't need to learn how to cook because she was so beautiful that she'd marry the governor and she could hire a cook. But my mother married my father, a policeman, and we had to make do with her inventive cooking.

Although it was already two months since Passover, my mother was making matzoh brei with the leftover matzoh in the house. Her original recipe.

"People who follow recipes are anal retentive," she'd say, as she threw in some farmer cheese, applesauce or raisins. I ate, but whenever a Betty Crocker commercial came on TV, I was ready to trade my mother for one of those moms who baked cakes, fussed over the laundry, and kept a neat house.

Our dishes didn't match and my mother set a scattershot table, plopping forks and knives in a heap. But there were daisies in a vase, and she wore lipstick and a bright scarf in her hair.

Mom put some matzoh brei on a plate for herself and sat down at the kitchen table with a copy of the *New York Daily Mirror*.

"That *f'shtinkener* should drop dead, dumping a lovely girl like that."

I went in and sat down next to her.

"Mommy, you're talking to yourself."

She looked at me.

"Justinele. My little queenele."

"What are you reading about?"

"That Eddie Fisher. A few years ago he divorced Debbie Reynolds to go run off with Elizabeth Taylor. Debbie Reynolds hasn't gotten over it."

I took a daisy out of the vase and put it behind her ear.

"Here, Mom, you could use a touch of color."

She laughed. "You're funny, you know that?" She kissed me on the cheek, and I instinctively rubbed at the red lipstick left behind.

"Speaking of *f'shtinkener* men, you didn't get your father a Father's Day present, did you?"

"Uh, no."

"He's lucky I even let you kids see him on Father's Day. Jake didn't get him a present, did he?"

"I don't think so," I said. I got up and left.

As I walked toward my room Jake whispered to me.

"Justine, get in here."

The boys had matching multicolored woven covers on their beds, but otherwise the room reflected their two completely different personalities. On his side, Jake had a bookshelf full of Batman and Superman comic books and *Mad* magazines, and a box of baseball cards. Leo had a desk with a Bronx High School of Science banner over it; his schoolbooks; a 1960 set of the *Book of Knowledge;* his acoustic guitar; and songbooks of The Weavers and Peter, Paul and Mary.

Jake sat cross-legged on his bed wearing his black-rimmed glasses and striped pajama bottoms with no top because it was already getting hot. At eleven, he was six years older than me, and anything he did was important. At that moment, he was making a card, drawing an intricate picture of interlocking cubic shapes in purple, blue, red, and orange with colored pencils.

I sat close to him as he read out loud: "Dear Dad, Happy Father's Day, Love, Jake."

"It's beautiful," I whispered. "Will you marry me?"

I glanced at Leo asleep in his bed. He had the sheet pulled over his face so only his black curly hair was visible. I didn't want to hurt his feelings but Jake was closer to my age and he played with me more.

"No," Jake said, although I could tell he was flattered. "You know brothers and sisters can't do that."

Quietly, he shut the bedroom door and pulled a gift-wrapped bottle of Old Spice aftershave from his dresser drawer.

"Look, I got Dad a present for Father's Day. If you chip in a dime or something you can sign the card."

"Mom would be mad if she found out."

"Well, she won't. Anyway, what's the big deal?"

"Leo didn't sign it."

"That's because he's afraid."

"Watch it," Leo said, no longer trying to sleep.

"It's true."

Leo threw off his sheet and sat up, frowning. "Shut up."

"Stop it," I said.

Jake put his hand on my shoulder. "Juz, you want to give Dad something for Father's Day, don't you?"

I nodded.

"So, just sign it. You only have to give me a nickel."

I found a pink pencil and carefully wrote my name.

"Troublemaker," Leo said as he got up and left the room. His hair, piled on top of his head from sleeping, looked a little goofy, but Leo was handsome. He had a high forehead, very white even teeth (the work of orthodontia, back when Dad lived with us) and a strong chin. When he smiled his whole face lit up but he wasn't smiling right now. He wandered into the kitchen and sat down.

Mom greeted him. "Hi, honey."

She put some matzoh brei in front him as Jake and I followed. Jake grabbed a plate, spooned a load of matzoh brei on it and moved toward the TV set.

"Don't you dare," Mom said. She wanted Jake to eat at the table.

Jake and Mom stared at each other. Jake didn't let the fact that Leo was her favorite stop him from claiming his share of attention. I loved him for that. Now he sat down at the kitchen table and I joined him. Mom scraped the last of the matzo brei on a plate for me.

"So, you're going to the beach."

"Yeah," I said.

"Your father and I went to Venice Beach in California on our honeymoon. Have I ever shown you the pictures?"

"Only about a million times," Jake said.

"I love those pictures," I said.

"Want to look at them again?"

"Okay."

The boys looked at each other and in one movement they grabbed their plates and headed for the TV. They settled onto the couch and tuned into an *I Love Lucy* rerun.

Mom opened a photo album and I sat next to her as she leafed through the pages of black and white photographs stuck on with self-adhesive corners. There was the graduation photo of her in a Hunter College cap and gown, the first girl in her extended family to go to college. Her parents had come to America from Russia and Latvia as teenagers, and her mother learned English and got her high school diploma. At Hunter, my mother took classes in psychology and education, but recalled proudly that she didn't study hard, not like that grind Joyce Bauer, who later became Dr. Joyce Brothers. Instead, my mother would leave classes early to wander the halls, socializing and starting clubs.

She's gorgeous in a honeymoon photo in Los Angeles, sporting a wide-brim hat and hooking arms with my father in his army uniform. Orson Welles noticed her when my parents toured the RKO studio, and arranged a screen test for her.

"Here we are in the commissary. See, Mommy had thin thighs then."

"Mom, do you think you and Daddy will ever get back together?"

"Would you like that?"

"Yeah."

"Well, Daddy and I are divorced now."

"I know that. Do people ever get undivorced?"

"Sometimes. Why don't you ask Daddy about it?"

I rested my cheek on my mother's arm.

"See what you can do," she said.

My father picked us up at ten sharp, as he did every Sunday morning. He stepped out of the car wearing sunglasses; a navy blue cap covered his balding head, and at first he seemed too tall and remote. Then he kissed me on the cheek and bent down to hug me. It came back to me then, that feeling of closeness to him. I had to relearn that every time I saw him. He kissed Jake while shaking his hand, and then did the same with Leo. Jake had explained to me that a lot of fathers stop kissing their sons after they reach a certain age, and he was glad that Dad still kissed him and Leo.

We handed Dad our bathing suits, and he put them in the trunk of the old Rambler where the rest of his things were carefully packed. He always brought towels for us, each towel neatly rolled up in two rubber bands, and he had everything else we might need in an emergency: not just jumper cables and a funnel to change the oil, but a canteen filled with water, paper towels, a sweater folded up small in a plastic bag with rubber bands and marked "sweater," a wool cap, also wrapped in plastic, clean cloths to be used as rags, tissues, a baseball cap, a spare towel, a knife packed in cardboard marked "utility knife," string, and a deck of cards.

On the way to the beach I counted three rabbits in the grass along the road. Dad drove with both hands on the steering wheel, often commenting on how important it was to stay two hundred feet behind the car in front of us and explaining other rules of the road.

Dad believed in obeying laws, and the boys loved to pump him with questions about what he knew and what he thought about things.

"Where's your gun, Dad?"

He had been a police captain and the boys remembered when he kept his policeman's revolver in his top dresser drawer at home. Years later, he told me he kept his gun for decades after he left the force in case my mother tried to commit an act of violence against his second wife, Gisela.

When we got to the Jones Beach parking lot Dad made sure we all helped carry stuff. In the bathhouse, I changed into my red, black and white checked bathing suit with the ruffles. Then Dad rented a giant striped umbrella from the stand, and we began trooping across the huge expanse of hot sand to find a spot. We passed teenagers lying in the sun listening to "Surf City" on transistor radios, children making sand castles, women with sun reflectors perched on their chests.

My father pointed out that the land around the beach was unspoiled by development, that the bathhouses were clean, that there was a first-aid station, well-run swimming pools and concession stands. We learned that Jones Beach was opened to the public in 1929, when my father was eleven. He admired reformers like Mayor LaGuardia and FDR; it thrilled him when the government and institutions worked well for the people.

"We'll set up here." Dad put down his load and began digging a hole for the umbrella. "Lend a hand, boys!"

He used big, jerky movements, overreacting to the chore. We thought it was comical, but the boys knelt down and helped dig the hole anyway and when it was deep enough, I held the umbrella in place while they filled up the hole with sand and packed it tight.

"Well done!" said Dad. "Next, the blanket!"

Dad unfolded the blanket and carefully laid it next to the umbrella.

"Okay, now secure the corners!"

We quickly put our sneakers on the corners.

This is what it was like with Dad. When he took us fishing, he made sure we all had fishing rods and the right bait. If we went to the movies, he bought us popcorn. He always paid full fare wherever we went and never tried to cheat.

After we had set up our things nicely, Dad took me by the hand and we went to the water. He showed me how to do strokes and kick my legs, holding me in his strong arms in the shallow water as I practiced.

Then came lunch. Dad laid out a tablecloth and opened a meticulously packed straw picnic basket. Inside were sandwiches that he'd made, neatly wrapped in waxed paper and labeled.

"What have we here? Tuna on white! Who's for tuna on white? Going once, going—"

"Me, Dad," one of us would say.

"There's a taker. Now, bologna on rye with mustard...."

He'd hand out the rest of the sandwiches and pour out cups of cold lemonade from his thermos, patting dry any drops that fell. He had a Tupperware container filled with perfect ten-minute hard-boiled eggs marked "HB" on the shells, as well as a little shaker with salt and pepper. There were celery and carrot sticks in plastic bags and for dessert a Sara Lee pound cake. His attention to these details seemed fanatical to me even as I was mesmerized by it. Before you ate you set up everything nicely; you had regular food first, dessert afterwards. When we finished eating, he made sure we "policed" the area, to pick up every scrap of paper we may have left behind.

The meritocracy of the police force, how you advanced through the ranks based on exams, suited Dad, although he didn't feel a kinship with the majority of cops. He felt he had to hide the fact that he was a liberal, that he deplored the racism and police brutality he witnessed in the police force at that time.

After lunch we helped Dad put the leftover food away. Then Leo picked up his paperback of *Great Expectations* and started reading. That's when Jake took out the card and gift-wrapped bottle of Old Spice aftershave. He was getting ready to give it to Dad when I suddenly remembered I was supposed to try to get Dad back together with Mom.

I put my hand on my father's arm. "Daddy, do you think you and Mommy—"

"Justine!" Jake glared at me. "Are you nuts?" He turned to Dad. "Dad, we got you a little Father's Day gift." Jake handed the present to Dad.

My father took the present and turned it around in his hands. He put his hand on Jake's shoulder.

"This is really nice. Thank you, Jake," said Dad, as he carefully opened the gift wrap. "Just what I use."

"And I made you a card, Dad." Jake smiled bashfully as he showed the card.

My father took it. "Jake, you made this?" He patted Jake on the head, as he read it. "It's really nice."

Dad sighed. "Listen, Jake, Justine, Leo, there's no good time to tell you this. I've been meaning to tell you...." He looked down, hesitating. "Kids, there's something important I have to talk to all of you about. I met a nice woman."

He had our full attention. "And, well, I'm getting married." His eyes kept darting around, without looking at us.

At first I didn't understand. I thought he meant he was marrying my mother again.

"Her name is Gisela. She has four sons. You'll like her."

We were quiet on the way home. I was in shock, not so much that Dad was going to marry another woman, but that he would be living with other children instead of us. I didn't want to think about Dad with those other kids, because when I did I imagined that they were better than us, that their lives were organized.

Leo sat in the front, his arms folded, staring out the window. Jake sat next to me in the back, his brown eyes melty with sadness. I wanted to comfort him and was amazed when he mustered up the spirit to ask Dad a question.

"How old are her sons?" Jake asked.

Leo turned around to face Jake, his face contorted. "Who cares? What difference does it make?"

"The twins, Harry and Billy, are eleven. Lloyd is ten, Ray is nine," Dad said.

That was all the information we could take. They weren't older, leading lives of their own. Dad would be like a father to them. At least I was the only girl and the youngest.

When we got to Queensview, Leo just took off upstairs without kissing Dad goodbye. Jake and I took our kiss from Dad, who tried to make us feel better by giving us hugs. It did make me feel better.

I don't remember who told Mom, but she took the eight-by-eleven sepia wedding photo from her dresser and smashed it on the floor.

"That miserable son of a bitch." Her voice sounded unnaturally deep, not like herself.

"Mom, take it easy," Leo said.

The boys and I were standing close together and she saw how frightened we were.

"Okay, okay."

Jake went for the broom and shovel and started to sweep up the glass.

"Be careful," Mom said. Leo helped Jake clean it all up.

"He's got his concubine. Well, I've got you kids. That's one thing he can't take away from me."

My mother drifted away to the TV and sank into the couch. Patti Page was on *The Ed Sullivan Show* singing "So In Love With You Am I."

I went to her closet and took out her pink cocktail dress with the sequins that she wore on special occasions. I brought it to her.

"Mom, do you want to put on your dress? It'll make you feel like a glamour girl," I said.

"Not tonight."

In the months that followed, Mom alternately slept a lot and was restless. She took me to Manhattan more and more. One night when we came home the apartment was dark except for a dim light coming from the kitchen.

"Boys? What's going on?"

In the kitchen Leo and Jake were doing their homework by the light of a Yahrzeit candle, the kind of candle we lit on the anniversaries of our grandparents' deaths.

"Forget to pay the electricity bill, Mom?" Jake pointed at the Yahrzeit candle like he was stabbing it.

"Not really. This place is a dumping ground for first wives. We're leaving. We may be moving to Manhattan."

"What?!"

"You kids don't know what I could really do if I had a chance. I could go to cocktail parties—"

"Yeah, yeah."

Mom started singing a Patti Page song, pretending she had a microphone in her hand.

We were waltzin' together to a dreamy melody
When they called out 'Change partners'
And you waltzed away from me.

We saw Dad a few more Sundays after that, until the day Mom locked Jake in the bathroom. She had been packing up our stuff, and the living room was cluttered with cardboard boxes filled haphazardly with our books and other possessions.

I was leaning out the window, waiting to see Dad's car pull up. The yentas were outside on their beach chairs when he arrived and got out of the car, expecting to see us. He looked up at me.

Inside the bathroom, Jake yelled and pounded the door, "Mom! Let me out! God damn it, Mom! Let me out of here!"

Mom paced around, excited. "I'll let you out soon. It's for your own good, Jake!"

Feeling daring, I yelled out the window so my father would know we were home.

"Daddy!"

Mom grabbed me and pulled me away from the window. "Whose side are you on?"

From inside his room, Leo slammed the door shut, loudly strumming his guitar.

The intercom buzzed and Mom triumphantly went to it.

"What do you want?"

"Where are the kids?" Dad asked from the intercom downstairs.

"You want the kids? Give us more money."

There was a pause.

"That's cruel, Martha."

"Well, you know all about cruelty, don't you?"

"This is crazy, Martha. Don't make the kids suffer because of trouble between us."

"You've got money to pay for your concubine. You can cough up money for the woman who's raising your children.

"I send you a check every damn week. I can't afford any more!"

"You've got a car," she said. "Sell it."

I rushed to the bathroom and pulled away the chair that was holding the door shut. Jake burst out and ran out of the house.

By the time Jake reached the sidewalk Dad's car was just disappearing up the street. Jake ran out and into the street; the yentas watched.

"He left, Jake," one of the ladies said. "Your father was here, and he waited. Then he left."

"Why didn't you come down?" asked the other one. "You keep your father waiting like that—"

But she stopped when the other lady elbowed her in the ribs. Jake stood at the curb.

The day the moving men came Mom was humming happily as she tossed clothes and small items into a box. A moving man carried a box with crystal goblets clinking against each other as he walked. He stopped.

"You might want to pack this up a little more carefully, ma'am. These things are likely to break."

"That's my wedding china. Who cares? When we're living in Manhattan I'll buy some more."

"I'll pack it up better, Mom," I offered. The moving man put the box down and I knelt down and carefully wrapped each crystal goblet in newspaper. But my mother was right not to pack carefully, because we never saw any of our possessions again. It was all sent off to a distant place, "storage" and she never reclaimed it. For years I used to imagine that my toy box and my dolls, and all our furniture and family photos were waiting for us in a huge, dusty warehouse somewhere.

Chapter 2.

Gypsies

Five years later we were living in a single room with a bathroom in the Empire Hotel, on West Sixty-Third Street near Lincoln Center. My mother and Leo slept on twin beds, and Jake and I slept on cots. It was our tenth hotel, my fourth school.

Leo, now nineteen, was a junior at City College, and Jake, sixteen, was a junior at Brandeis High School. The boys helped out with part-time jobs, Jake at Bartons Chocolate Shop on Seventy-Second Street, and Leo as a messenger. They contributed money to the family, but also kept a bit for themselves for school lunch, subway fares, and occasionally haircuts—though they tended to wait as long as possible before spending money on a haircut. Jake's glasses were thicker than Leo's, and Jake was slightly husky, but to me, both of my brothers looked ideal. They dressed like the Smothers Brothers with a bit of the Kingston Trio thrown in.

Of all the places we stayed in, the Empire felt the most like home. We lived there for a comparatively long time, a year, and then we left and came back for another six months. Lincoln Center was being built when we moved in, and I used to ride my bicycle all around the plaza, before the fountain had water, until it was nearly finished and the guards told me I couldn't ride there anymore.

In May of 1966 I began sleepwalking. One night, when everyone else was asleep, I fumbled in the half-light around the clutter of newspapers, strewn clothes, schoolbooks and shopping bags and found my blue pleated skirt. I didn't own pants, just a dress and a skirt that I alternated wearing. I put my skirt on over my nightgown, moving quietly so as not to wake up Jake and Leo. Leo slept deeply. He didn't smile easily, but when he did, his face lit up.

I needed to get outside quickly, urgently. I didn't even comb my hair. Just slipped on my worn brown penny loafers, picked up two shopping bags and opened the door to the hallway.

Downstairs the clerk at the front desk barely noticed me as I came out of the elevator and walked through the lobby. It was early in the morning, about five. As I crossed Broadway I didn't notice the cars until a taxi came around the corner and swerved to avoid me. I walked past the Sixty-Third Street Y, where we often had meals in the smelly cafeteria.

Back in the hotel room, Jake woke up, perhaps instinctively sensing something was wrong. Later he told me that when he realized I was missing, he woke Leo and my mother and quickly threw on some clothes. In the lobby he shouted to the front desk clerk, asking if he'd seen me. The clerk gestured outside.

Jake took our usual route, toward Central Park, running all the way. After half a block he could see me in the distance and he caught up with me as I was about to cross Central Park West.

"Where ya goin', shrimp?" He was out of breath as he grabbed me by the shoulders. At that moment, I realized I had been sleepwalking. The transition to consciousness was swift; it took only a second.

"I dreamed we were moving again."

"I know," he said.

Jake took the shopping bags and put his arm around me as we walked back to the hotel.

My mother was in the lobby, wearing a coat over her nightgown. As we came in, and the desk clerk could see that I was all right, he called to her.

"Mrs. Blau!"

"That *f'shtinkener*," my mother said under her breath, glaring at him. "He's gonna give me a hard time now."

He hesitated. "There's the problem of your bill. I'm afraid it's up to $150 at this point. We'd like to—"

"Can't you see that we're in a life or death emergency right now?"

He faltered. "Well, the manager asked me to speak..."

My mother turned her back on him. "Come, Justine. Are you okay?"

She put her arm around me, and we walked toward the elevator.

"What are we going to do with you?" Mom said to me. As we got in the elevator, she looked harshly at the clerk, as though what had happened was his fault.

"Be as dignified as possible," I thought to myself. "Show people you are respectable."

Back in the room, sunlight came through our northeast facing window. My socks and panties were drying on the radiator where I'd put them the night before after washing them. My mother opened the window and took a container of orange juice from the windowsill.

"Here, have some orange juice. It's healthy." She poured me half a glass. "Okay. Everything's going to be all right."

Jake was smoothing a comb through his hair, but at this he slammed it down on the dresser. "Gimme a break, lady. Your daughter sleepwalks all the way to Central Park, and you think giving her some orange juice makes everything all right?"

Leo turned on the TV. *Bullwinkle*, one of his favorite shows was on. He saw no point in arguing with her.

"It could be worse," my mother said to Jake. "The main thing is we have our health—"

"Mom, Justine sleepwalks because we're living in one room, and we don't have enough money. We never have enough money. Aren't you worried?"

"Am I worried? A little. But aside from the sleepwalking, Justine's fine. What do you expect, perfection? You think it would be so good for her to go back to a boring apartment building in Queens? And come home and watch television every night? And have a nice little mommy who stays home every day watching soap operas and making meat loaf?"

She walked into the bathroom to get dressed.

Jake didn't miss a beat, and he shouted at the closed door.

"That's just what she needs! We *liked* living in Queens. We had all our friends. We had a real kitchen. And we went to the same school every year. Justine, how many schools have you been in since we left Queens?"

"Four."

"Four. Four schools in four years. How many hotels have we lived in during those four years, Martha?"

He called her "Martha" whenever he was berating her. She looked chastened; she knew she had to take this verbal beating.

"The Taft," he began. That was the first hotel we lived in. "Then 1360 York Avenue." He started counting on his fingers. "The boardinghouse in the Bronx. The Hotel Wellington. The Chesterfield on 50th Street. The Empire for a year. The Westover on 72nd Street. Then the Excelsior on 81st Street. The apartment on 56th Street. The Broadmoor on 102nd Street.

"Then there was the night we walked the streets all night and sat in all-night diners. Then back to the Empire. It's a *shonda*," he said, throwing her lingo back at her. "Shame on you."

My mother came out of the bathroom and the downcast Martha was gone.

"All three of you do well in school," she said brightly. "So what's the problem? Jakey, boy, you have to appreciate what you have. We go to concerts in the park, we go to museums, lectures. We go to movies. Hey, I've got great kids. You've got a great mother. We're on top of the world!"

She went back in the bathroom. We could hear her talking to herself.

"One day they'll look back on these times and laugh."

Leo looked around. "Is there any orange juice left?"

Jake shook the carton and tossed it into the garbage.

"Any milk for cereal?" Leo asked.

Jake went to the windowsill and smelled the milk. He made a face. Leo scooped a handful of Rice Krispies out of the box and ate some. I sat next to him on the bed and reached for the box. The three of us took turns scooping out the Rice Krispies.

When she came back in the room, we looked at her.

"You kids. You're always hungry." She looked at her reflection in the mirror over the dresser. "All right, I've got it." She did a little impromptu waltz step. "Let's live a little. We're going to get chopped liver, challah, some schnapps, caviar, the works."

It was a Saturday morning, so my mother's idea of saving the day was to find a synagogue that had a Bar Mitzvah going on and join in on the kiddush. Sometimes a kiddush is just *rugelach* and coffee, but if the family hosting it can afford to be generous, the Kiddush is a feast. We walked through the park to Temple Emanuel on Sixty-Fifth Street and Fifth Avenue. We used to go to the Sutton Place Synagogue on Fiftieth Street near Third Avenue and the Central Synagogue on Lexington Avenue and 55th Street; but we'd burned our bridges in those places, so now we were going to try this one.

In the sanctuary a Bar Mitzvah was ending—a boy was singing his Haftorah portion. The women in the congregation wore mink stoles, diamond rings, and the kind of clothes I saw in store windows. I searched for the preteen girls in the congregation and studied the way they were dressed. It wasn't just the Mary Janes or the mod styles or black velvet headbands over flipped hair—it was the way they carried themselves, like they owned the place.

Finally, the cantor rose. "And now the Spiegel family is hosting a kiddush downstairs. Their guests and the congregation are invited. *Mazel tov.* Good *Shabbos.*"

Organ music played as people stood up and began filing out. We joined the crowd and went down the stairs too.

"Mom, we don't even know these people." I knew our shab-biness must be conspicuous, and I wondered if we'd be noticed and questioned.

"What do they care if a hungry family eats a little? It's a *mitz-vah* for them to provide some food. They should thank us."

The buffet table was heaped with platters of lox and white fish, bagels, salads, trays of fruit and pastries. Nobody touched anything until the rabbi came downstairs and said the blessing over the chal-lah.

"Baruch atah adonoy, eloheynu melech haolum, amosei lechem min haaretz."

The rabbi pulled a piece of challah and had a bite, and said the blessing for the wine. As soon as people started eating, we joined the line at the buffet table where Mom handed me a plate. Most people stood around talking and eating, but we sat at a table in the corner and dug in. I was so hungry I could barely manage to wait to spread the cream cheese and layer it with lox, a rare treat.

An elegant older couple sat down next to us, and Mom nod-ded demurely to them. After awhile, Leo said to Mom in an English accent, "Are you and Father dining at Lutèce tonight?" The four of us laughed quietly.

"You see? Life is always an adventure," Mom said.

After we ate, Mom took a rose out of the flower arrangement on the buffet table and tucked it into her hair. I looked around but no one had noticed.

"How do I look?"

The only one who would indulge her was Leo. "Nice, Mom."

She was satisfied. "Come, Justine, help me pack up some food to take home."

"Mom, no!"

"Look at all this leftover food. They're just going to throw it away."

"I'll wait for you outside."

Out in the lobby some girls about my age were giggling together. To avoid them I wandered into the cloakroom and ran my hand along the luxurious softness of the furs hanging there when the thought occurred to me: *One of these coats could help us get an apartment.*

My great-grandfather, my mother's grandfather, had been a melamed, a scholar who trains boys for their Bar Mitzvahs. My mother explained that he stayed home and studied and didn't earn much money, so he sent his son, my grandfather, to work as a field hand in an orchard at nine years old instead of going to school. My grandfather came to America as a teenager and met my mother's mother, Rose, from Minsk, who had witnessed pogroms as a girl.

My mother was born at home on Ninety-Eighth Street and Second Avenue in 1920. The family had a hat store around the corner, and when my mother was a little girl she used to bring a kettle of tea down to her father in the store. Her parents worked long hours and she spent a lot of time in the store.

My grandfather had movie-star looks, and my mother got her sparkling eyes and aquiline nose from him.

"My father would dance around the store with me, my toes would be on his toes. That's where I got socialized," my mother remembered. She said that all babies are cute but she was extremely cute. So she got accustomed to compliments at an early age.

Jake came up beside me. "Dukes up." I lifted my fists and got into boxer's stance, like he had taught me. He feigned a punch but I blocked him.

"Good," he said, getting in a soft slap on my face. "Cover your face!"

I raised my arms and tried to get a punch in, but he blocked me.

Later that afternoon Leo went to his part-time job making deliveries for a liquor store. Back in our room my mother put on red nail polish. An Indonesian ambassador she'd met had told her about a cocktail party at his embassy. Maybe Mom could get an autograph for the book she was writing, *Golden Quotations on the United Nations*. Jake was getting ready to go to a party at Kenny Beigeleisen's house, his friend from Wagner Junior High School. He had borrowed an iron from the hotel chambermaid and was ironing a white shirt on the bed.

"Jake, take your sister to the party."

"I'm not bringing her to my party. *You* take her. You're the mother." Jake turned the shirt and expertly ironed a sleeve.

"Don't get fresh. A little responsibility won't kill you."

Jake shook his head. "Look who's talking about responsibility! People are supposed to pay their bills, but you don't."

"That's different. God says, 'Life before Torah.' We have to get by."

Jake unbuttoned the shirt he was wearing and put on the clean white one. He was a little pudgy and his stomach strained the top of his pants.

"Well, I have to get by too," Jake said, carefully keeping the zipper of his pants in place with a safety pin. "And God knows, after putting up with you, I'm entitled to have a good time at a party without dragging my sister along."

"Respect your mother and in the long run you'll be better off." It was settled. She turned to me. "Remember Justine, don't tell anyone our business. If they ask where we live, just say we're—"

"I know. We're in between apartments."

"Come on, lady." Jake yanked the iron cord out of the outlet. "I have enough to put up with."

Instantly Mom shifted into an angry realm.

"Don't aggravate me!" she yelled, her voice deep. "What are you, a roughneck? You're taking her to the party and that's that."

Jake sneered at me. I shrugged, thrilled that I would get to go along.

We walked passed the Heckscher Playground where I had learned how to play knock hockey and where Jake had won a trophy for the playground spin top competition. He went on to compete in the borough-wide contest and came in fifth. We passed the giant mica-flecked boulder that I had climbed dozens of times. Behind the playground was the path where my father had taught me to ride a bicycle, the one he gave me for my eighth birthday.

We approached Kenny's house, whistling the theme from *The Andy Griffith Show*.

As we stood outside his friend's apartment house, a white highrise doorman building on East Sixty-Seventh Street, we heard the song *Winchester Cathedral* playing inside. Kenny, a John-John Kennedy lookalike even though he was Jewish, opened the door. Behind him kids were dancing and fooling around.

"Hey, man." Jake and Kenny punched each other.

"Happy birthday." Jake handed Kenny a copy of *Mad* magazine. "I got you this. It's not much but—"

"Thanks! I haven't read this one yet." Kenny knew something about Jake's circumstances. He stood aside to let Jake in but Jake hesitated.

"Um, Kenny, I was kind of forced to bring...my sister."

Kenny looked at me.

"That's okay."

Inside that apartment was a different world. Afternoon light came in from high windows on two sides. Teenagers were flirting on soft leather couches. I took in the wall-to-wall carpeting, the glass coffee table, the framed photos in the bookshelves—it was a wonderland. These people must be so happy here, I thought.

"Go take some soda if you want," Jake said to me, before ditching me for good.

I went to the snack table and poured a cup of 7UP.

"Here comes the mysterious Jake Blau," one of the kids said.

"So where are you living now, Jake?"

"Classified information, hombre."

I stepped out onto the terrace and marveled at the fourteenth-floor view of Third Avenue. In the distance I could even see Central Park.

I went back for food when a tan Cocker Spaniel poked its head out of the kitchen and headed straight under the snack table.

I fed the dog a cracker with paté and petted it. The dog was licking my hand, hoping for more, when an older woman with an Eastern European accent called out, "Pushkin! Where are you?" The dog hid under the table, as a kindly-looking lady in her late seventies wearing a housedress came out. She looked incongruous in this household.

"Pushkin, come out of there." She looked at me.

"Can you get the dog for me? He won't bite."

Of course! Justine to the rescue. I reached under the table, and gently pulled the dog out.

"This dog, he'll eat all the hors d'oeuvres. I have to watch him every minute," she told me.

"I'll watch him for you."

She looked at me and realized I was younger than the others.

"That would be a big help, *bubeleh*. Bring him in the kitchen, and you can keep me company while I make some more hors d'oeuvres."

The dog and I followed her to the kitchen, the kind of kitchen you saw in commercials, with lots of counter space. More bowls of chips and pretzels were on the counter, refills for the ones in the living room.

"So, who are you?" She put some pretzels and miniature frankfurters wrapped in pastry on a plate.

"I'm just the sister of one of Kenny's friends," I explained. "My mother made him bring me."

"Well, I'm glad she did. It's nice to have some company in here." She gestured toward the kitchen door. "Teenagers never seem to have time for their old grandmothers. Would you like a little something to eat?"

I nodded and she put a hot dog in front of me.

"Sit here, sweetie." Sweetie. That sounded like something Midwestern women said. I sat down.

"I wish I had a grandmother."

"Oh, you don't have one?"

I shook my head. "Well, technically I do. But she's on my father's side, and my mother doesn't let us see her."

"That's a shame."

I took a bite. "It's good. Thank you Mrs...?"

"Just call me Nana." She nodded toward the food. "So, you like it?"

"Yeah."

The dog sat in front of me, eyeing my frankfurter. I held my arm up, dangling it over him before tossing him a piece.

"Oh, your dress is torn."

"Yeah. My mother forgot to sew it. I'll remind her tonight."

Nana came over to take a look at the rip under the armpit.

"The dress is too small on you. But I can fix it. Take it off, and I'll sew it."

"No, that's okay. Really."

But she gently prodded me and handed me a robe to put on. I went into her little bedroom next to the kitchen and took off the dress.

As Nana worked some magic on the dress, I forgot I wasn't supposed to talk about our circumstances.

"My mother says she's gonna get her book published. But I wish we could just get an apartment back in Queens. Rents are cheaper there, you know, and then we could get by on the money from my father. And it wouldn't matter so much if my mother didn't work."

Nana nodded sympathetically. "Your mother sounds like a fascinating woman. But when a woman has children, sometimes it's better for her to be not so fascinating for awhile."

She handed the dress to me. "Here you go, sweetie."

Sweetie again.

I put on the dress as she continued. "You're a strong girl, I can see that. Maybe you and your brothers can make her understand; the important thing is to have a nice home. So what if it's in Queens?"

She stroked my hair. "I been living in Manhattan for twenty years. It's not so hot."

The following morning, Sunday, the phone woke us up at about eight. Leo answered it and immediately scowled.

"Maybe you should talk to my mother," Leo said into the phone. He covered the mouthpiece. "The guy at the desk says we have to pay a hundred dollars or get out. Otherwise they'll confiscate our possessions."

"Here we go again," said Jake.

"Mom, I've got a calculus exam tomorrow," said Leo. "I've got to stay here."

"Tell him I'm coming down. I'll handle this," she said, putting on her clothes. "Come with me, Justine."

"If you're handling it, why do I have to come?"

"You know why," she said. I did. I was her foil, the nice little girl who kept people from arguing with her.

Downstairs, the manager was waiting for her. My mother turned on the charm. "How are you?" she beamed.

"Fine."

"I understand we have a problem," she said. "You've been very patient. Would you be kind enough to give us a day or two to catch up with the rent?"

"If you can't settle this bill, I gotta ask you to leave. Hotel policy."

"Let me speak to the manager."

"I am the manager."

She made one final attempt.

"The children have school tomorrow. Just a day or two longer."

He hesitated and I willed him to see how worthy we were.

"My brother has to study for an exam tomorrow. He's in college." You don't kick nice kids out.

He shook his head and looked away from me. "Sorry, but it's out of the question."

She stared at him a long time to make him uncomfortable. "Top of the day to you," she said, and we walked away.

When we returned to the hotel room, she broke the news to the boys. "Let's go. We're packing up."

"I can't," Leo said.

"I'll write you a note."

"A note? Not for college, you don't."

"Mom, did you negotiate with the manager?" Jake asked.

"I didn't like his manner, that little punk. As soon as they find out you're a little short of cash, they get nasty. We'll show 'em, right boys?"

Leo tried to take some control. "Mom, did you offer them some money?"

She spoke gently to Leo. "We'll manage, honey. We just have to get through tonight."

"C'mon, Mom." Jake wasn't being belligerent; he was pleading. "Don't do this again."

She looked at him firmly. "Ask not what your mother can do for you. Ask what you can do for your mother."

We started off that night walking over to the newsreel theater in Times Square, the four of us with ten shopping bags. On the way, a couple of Gypsy kids carrying a bucket of roses thrust a single rose at us. "A rose for your girlfriend, one dollar," they said. Leo shook his head, but I couldn't stop staring at them. They didn't go to school, nobody made sure they got a good night's sleep; and their mothers tried to entice people into their storefront salons on side streets to have their fortunes told.

I was proud that the Gypsy kids tried to sell roses to us, because it meant that we fooled them. They thought we were the kind of people who could spare a dollar for a rose. They didn't know that we were more like them than tourists. The Gypsy kids and my brothers and I understood what the tourist kids didn't: the world is a tough, unfair place, people are selfish, and you have to try to get out of life what you can.

It was cheaper to see black-and-white newsreels than a regular movie, a buck fifty, but even so, Mom bought only two tickets.

"Hey, there are four of you," the usher said.

"We have two tickets. The manager lets us." My mother pushed me forward and the boys followed closely.

"Well, I have to ask him. I can't just let you go in."

"Two tickets are fine," my mother said, walking by him, winking at him as if they're both in on a secret.

"No, I can't do that."

"Come on, children," she said to us, and we followed her into the theater. I turned around. The ticket taker knew we'd cheated, but this wasn't a battle worth fighting.

The theater was only a quarter full so we could rest our feet on the tops of the seats in front of us. Somebody snored behind us as we watched a newsreel about Princess Margaret. After an hour Leo and I went downstairs to the lounge. He sat on a red vinyl couch studying for his abnormal psychology test while I stuck my hand inside the popcorn machine. Under the metal grate that the cup rested on was a space where popcorn that didn't make it into the cup fell. I squeezed my hand in and could get some. I got some for Leo, too, then lay down next to him and slept.

When they started vacuuming up at one in the morning, we had to leave. Outside we stood around with our shopping bags.

"Okay, lady, now what?" Jake scowled.

"Assess the situation and act accordingly," my mother said.

We started walking toward Central Park, passing the red neon sign in the window of a pub: a horse's tail swishing left and right, left and right. I was so tired. As we trudged to the park, I thought longingly of having a small apartment with a rocking chair and a rug. We entered the park at Sixty-Third Street and took over a curved line of benches. My mother sat up and by the light of a lamppost perused *Golden Quotations on the United Nations.* She'd been working on the book for years, filling a large scrapbook with photographs and quotations about peace from politicians and United Nations dignitaries, like Eleanor Roosevelt, Dag Hammarskjold, and Golda Meir. Her favorite quotation was from Adlai Stevenson, her idol:

"All progress has resulted from people who took unpopular positions."

Mom hand-wrote the quotations with gold ink. She thought when she got this book published she'd make money.

It would be years before I learned it is a frequent characteristic of bipolar people to think they have a connection with the United Nations or other world peace organizations. My brothers and I didn't know then that she was bipolar; we didn't know what bipolar was. But we did know that her book was a fruitless endeavor.

I lay down with my head in my mother's lap. The boys lay down too, using shopping bags for pillows.

My mother kind of talked to herself as she leafed through her book.

"You see, you don't have to be rich to enjoy life. Alternatives, always think of alternatives. That's what's wrong with most people. They're afraid to take risks, to have a little adventure.

"Above all, never lose hope. I might get my book published. Maybe your father will sell his car and give us the money. Who knows? I might meet someone who appreciates my ideas. Anything could happen."

She began singing and humming Brahms's Lullaby. "Lullaby, and good night, la la laa laa…"

I was grateful to escape into sleep.

Chapter 3.

My Mother and the Concubine

The next morning I knew from the green wooden slats of the bench I was sleeping on that we were in Central Park. I heard pigeons moseying around and the cars on Central Park West stopping at traffic lights. A Gimbels shopping bag was under my head for a pillow. My mother had moved me off her lap during the night so she could lie down too.

As I sat up I saw Jake reach for his glasses and put them on.

My mother's varicose veins and the garters holding her beige stockings were showing.

"Mom, pull your dress down," I said, and she did.

I had my navy blue button-down sweater on, and my mother had put one of her blouses over me to keep me warm, but I was a little stiff. A couple of people passed by us walking their dogs, and I tried to straighten out my rumpled clothes. I prayed that I wouldn't see any kids.

We carried our stuff to the Sixty-Third Street Y, a couple of blocks away, to use the bathroom and get breakfast. As we walked over there, I leaned my head on Jake's shoulder and tried to walk with my eyes closed. I remembered how Leo and Jake used to carry me when I was younger, but I was ten now and that was out of the question.

Mom walked ahead with Leo.

"You're a good son and a great help to me." She reached up and smoothed down his thick curls with her fingers. "Everything's going to work out, believe me."

He adjusted the shopping bags to redistribute the weight.

In the Y, my mother and I went to the ladies' room, and Jake and Leo went to the men's room. I finally had a chance to scratch my behind in private. I had little white worms, about a quarter of an inch long, in my rectum. It didn't occur to me that a doctor could do anything about it, since we didn't go to doctors. Not on principle— we just didn't go. I didn't tell anyone about the worms, because I thought it was a shameful thing and my fault that I had them. I would scratch the itching when I could, embarrassed that I had to do it, look at the tiny white worm or two worms squirming on my finger and then thoroughly wash my hands. I thought this was the way things were—people had worms sometimes.

Mom and I washed our hands and faces, combed our hair and brushed our teeth. After we finished with the toothpaste I went out to the hallway and gave it to Jake so he and Leo could use it.

Mom put on lipstick and looked better. Despite being over-weight and broke, she was still pretty. She smiled at her reflection.

Only a few other people were in the cafeteria at seven, but it was nice to be in a warm, bright place that was operational and to be doing what we were supposed to be doing: eating breakfast. I was hungry and wished I could have had pancakes and eggs, but instead I had Cream of Wheat with milk, and the four of us shared two orange juices. As my mother drank her coffee and spread butter and grape jelly on her English muffin, she informed me I wasn't going to school that day.

"I'm taking you to see your father."

Disappointment slammed me. I disconnected inside to protect myself from hopelessness. "I want to go to school."

"We need to get some money from him."

"Mom, I don't want to do that!"

"It's important. The family needs you today, Justine."

I gave up.

She turned to the boys. They were downcast and didn't look her in the eyes. "We'll meet after school at the Donnell Library."

After we stored our bags in two lockers at the Y, Leo and Jake gave me a kiss on the cheek goodbye and I watched as they went off to school.

My mother and I took the subway down to Forty-Second Street, then the Number Seven to the East Side. She left me at the glass entrance of Hornblower & Weeks-Hemphill, Noyes, at Forty-First Street and Third Avenue. My father worked there as a stockbroker, whatever that was. The plan was for me to meet her around the corner at a coffee shop when I was done.

I pulled up my white knee socks before opening the door. My blue and green plaid dress with the white collar and three-quarter sleeves would have been fine if I hadn't been wearing it for three days in a row. I knew I didn't look good enough to be visiting my father at his office. At the far wall white numbers flitted electronically across a black screen. It was much too complicated for me to understand. I liked it better when he'd been a police captain. When anybody bothered me I told them my father was a policeman and he'd arrest them, and they'd leave me alone.

I approached the receptionist and asked for Mr. Blau.

"Mr. Blau, your daughter is here," she said into the phone. "Yes, here in the reception area."

She hung up. "He'll be right out, honey," she said to me. "No school today?"

I shrugged. I knew it would be ladylike to sit down and fold my hands but I couldn't sit still. My father would consider my visit troublesome. I hated to bother him.

My father had started City College when he was fifteen, but with younger brothers and sisters to help support, he had to leave college at eighteen to work. He once described to me how fervently he wished that he could have stayed in college.

In 1941 the New York City Police Department announced that the seven-year hiring freeze because of the Depression was over, and there were openings for 300 rookies. Some 29,000 men (and a few women) applied for the positions. My father trained rigorously to pass the physical, running every morning for miles on the beach at Coney Island, where his family lived at the time. He studied hard for the entrance exam and earned a spot in the Police Academy. I'd seen the newspaper clippings about that class of 1941, the best-educated class in the history of the police department. It also had more Jews than any other year—young men who were relieved to get a steady job after living through the Depression.

My father didn't talk much about his childhood because he didn't want to relive it. But we picked up bits and pieces of his life that explained why orderliness was so important to him. He grew up on the Lower East Side, the third boy of seven children. His father, Abraham, a factory worker, was smart but drank. My father never had a good word to say about him. At one point my grandfather had saved up his money, $2,000, to start an undertaking business, but he gambled at the racetrack and lost everything.

They were so poor they couldn't afford to go to the dentist; my father's nickname was Tootie because he had rotten teeth.

My father appeared. Tense smile.

"Justine."

He was tall and dignified in his gray suit. It always made me proud to see him.

"Hi Daddy." He gave me a kiss and a hug.

I followed him to his cubicle. On his desk was a large framed photo of a middle-aged woman with short blonde hair and blue eyes. I'd never met her, but I knew that was the Concubine, his second wife, Gisela. A few small school photos of my brothers and me were neatly pinned to the bottom of his bulletin board.

My father looked at me closely.

"Are you all right?" He was trying to assess how dire my situation was. It had been eight months since I'd seen him.

I nodded.

"It's good to see you, Justine. But shouldn't you be in school?"

"Yeah. But, Daddy, we need some money."

He sighed. "What happens to the money I send you?"

I imitated my mother with a Jewish intonation. "Money goes."

I thought I was funny, but he was incensed. "Money goes. Money goes when you stay in hotels instead of an apartment! When you eat in restaurants all the time instead of making meals. Where are you staying now?"

I looked away. I didn't know where he lived, but I imagined the home he shared with the Concubine was clean and neat.

"Justine, where are you staying?"

I looked back at him. "Mommy said not to tell you."

"Not to tell me? She won't tell me where my own children are sleeping at night?"

"Daddy—" He glared at me, and I capitulated.

"We slept in Central Park last night."

He looked as though he'd been hit.

"Don't worry, Dad. It's just temporary."

"My God." He rubbed his face with his thick hands. "Justine, you shouldn't have to go through this." He sighed as he pulled out his wallet. "She's really gone too far."

"Mommy said it was just for one night."

He nodded and counted out seventeen dollars and handed it to me.

"Give this to Mom."

I whispered, "Daddy, I think she wants more."

"I sent her the check. This is all I've got." His face got stern. "And you tell her this: She had better get an apartment and settle down soon. Or I'm going to family court."

My mother seethed for hours as we walked uptown. She erupted every once in awhile, "That miserable *pishika*. That lousy *cockala*."

People stared at her, frowning.

We stopped to use the bathroom at Rumplemeyer's, a fancy ice cream parlor on Central Park South. As we exited, a well-dressed pretty girl about my age came in with her father. There was something about the fluid, elegant way he held the door for her that struck me. In that fleeting moment, I understood that she was entitled and I wasn't. I was using the bathroom and she was having ice cream with her father.

I bet she had wall-to-wall carpeting, pink curtains in her bedroom, a pink princess phone, a dollhouse and precious tchotchkes that her mother arranged nicely, a bed with a flowered bedspread and matching sheets, a complete set of Laura Ingalls Wilders's *Little House* series in her bookshelves. She would have piano lessons and practice in the living room on a grand piano decorated with family photographs in silver frames.

We walked past the outdoor café on the corner of Seventh Avenue where the little round tables had bowls of complimentary peanuts. No waiter was in sight and my mother deftly took a handful of peanuts, scarcely missing a beat as we continued on. We smiled as she gave me half the peanuts. I knew what she was thinking. Life before Torah. It's just that our lives weren't at risk. To my mother's way of thinking, being a little hungry demanded immediate gratification, enabling her to rationalize a bit of pilfering.

"Mom, when I grow up I'm going to write a book about you."

She lit up. "What will it say?" She was fishing for compliments.

"That you taught your kids how to survive. And you always had a trick up your sleeve."

She savored the moment. "Are you going to share the profits with me?"

"Sure, Mom."

"That's my girl." She kissed me on the cheek.

That night, after we met the boys and picked up our stuff from the Y, we rode the subways. I had hoped for a miracle, but it was another night without a plan. I sat between my brothers, protected by them. My mother sat apart from us, in her own world, humming to herself. We rode the D train all the way out to Coney Island and back. On the way, Jake told me a story.

"Once upon a time there was a very rich man who lived in a big house in the suburbs, with a pool and a basketball court. He had a teenage son, Frank, who he loved very much.

"And the rich man had given Frank everything he wanted: a giant electric train set, a walkie-talkie set, even a Jaguar with white-wall tires."

Leo was listening too. We had the subway car mostly to ourselves. The train stopped at New Utrecht Avenue, Bay Parkway, Twenty-Fifth Avenue; and a tired person would get off or on.

Jake continued. "The trouble is, on Frank's sixteenth birthday the rich man couldn't think what to get him. The kid already had everything. The man thought and thought. Finally, he figured out what to do.

"The rich man bought 500 Hershey bars and melted them down. When the chocolate started to cool, he built a life-size sculpture of a man! The father worked on his statue very hard, and his chocolate man looked real. Finally, when he'd finished the statue, it looked so delicious he couldn't resist taking a bite out of the chocolate man's nose!"

I gasped.

"Suddenly, the chocolate man came alive! 'J'accuse!' he yelled. He clutched his nose and leaped to the mirror, where he saw that most of his nose was gone. Shouting, 'You will pay for this, hombre!' he dashed out the door, while the rich man was so surprised he couldn't move."

"Then what happened?"

"Well, my little chickadee, tune in next week; same time, same channel."

I rested my head on Jake's shoulder.

"Great story, hombre," Leo said, and Jake looked happy. When Leo gave a compliment, you knew you deserved it. I took Leo's hand and studied it. He had beautiful hands, strong yet finely shaped. Exactly how a young man's hands should be.

I was proud of Jake and Leo's stories, their jokes, their plaid shirts, top button open just like the Smothers Brothers, cleverly they explained the world to me. I took my brothers' love for granted; I thought they gave it freely. For a few minutes I felt like the richest girl in the world.

A few stops later Mom suggested that the four of us split up. "Leo and Jake, maybe the two of you should sleep in Penn Station tonight."

"And where are you two going?"

"Justine and I will get a single room. That's all I have money for."

I hated to be parted from the boys, and I hooked my arms through theirs.

Jake shook my arm off, bitterly.

"You realize, don't you, that Mom doesn't know what she's doing? We need help. Leo, what do you think?"

"I don't know."

"Am I the only sane one here? I think we should call Dad and ask him to help us."

Call Dad and ask for help. Not just for money out of his wallet, but to take care of us. Jake was brilliant. I began to think there was hope.

Meantime, the boys got off the train at Thirty-Fourth Street. Mom and I took it up to East Eighty-Sixth Street, to a dingy hotel that only charged ten dollars a night.

The hotel clerk wasn't going to rent it to us; a single room isn't supposed to be used for two people, but it was a piece of cake talking him into it. "Be nice. It's late already. My daughter has school tomorrow. She's a little girl and she's very sleepy."

"It's against the rules." But he slapped the room key on the desk.

"Room 44. Ten bucks. In advance."

Before walking in the room I hoped it would turn out to be better than I anticipated, but it was the usual; a twin bed with a drab green chenille bedspread, a tiny sink, a worn down dresser and chair.

"Okay. *Zay gezunt*," she said. "What can you do?"

I took off my dress and looked through the shopping bags until I found one of the boys' t-shirts to wear as pajamas.

While my mother went to the bathroom in the hall, I quickly brushed my teeth in the little sink. Then I washed my panties, using the tiny bar of soap. I wrung the panties out and hung them on the radiator to dry.

I heard my mother talking to herself as she walked back to the room. "When my aunt's house burned down my father gave her $4,000. But when I asked them for something, I got nothing."

We lifted the mattress off the box spring and put it on the floor for me to sleep on. I had the bottom sheet, and we tucked the top sheet around the box spring for Mom. Luckily for her, I wanted to have a back straight as an Indian, so I didn't use a pillow. She put the blanket over me and kissed me good night on the cheek.

The next morning it was raining. I picked up the phone and called the operator to find out what time it was. Then I shook my mother.

"Mom. Wake up! It's seven o'clock already! I have to go to school!"

"You don't have to go to school today. You had a hard night. It's not a good idea to knock yourself out."

"I'm going to school." I pulled the sheet off her.

"Stop it," she said, but she slowly sat up. "All right, I'm coming."

Because it was May, the radiator wasn't on. So my underwear and socks hadn't dried.

"Mom, my panties and socks are still wet!"

"Okay, so we'll wait until they're dry. Don't worry, you can be a little late."

"Now. We're going now, Mom. Get dressed."

"What a trooper you are."

Slowly I put on the panties, hating her every cold inch as I tried not to let the damp cloth touch my legs.

I had to wait until she had a shower. I hadn't had a shower in days, but I couldn't take a shower in that depressing place. Finally, we went outside and I was on my way to school, PS 59, on Fifty-Seventh Street.

"Come. Let's get on a bus. I'll explain to the driver that we don't have any money."

"No, Mom. I don't like it when you do that. We can walk to school."

But I really did want to ride the bus. A bus came and I hung back, so maybe people wouldn't realize I was with her.

She just whispered to the driver, and he waved us in. I relaxed a little before school. After a while someone got off, and I sat down.

"I'll bring you something nice at lunch," my mother said.

At lunchtime in the cafeteria I sat near the door so Mom could find me. I had a hard time keeping my eyes off Paul Kaplan's thick roast beef sandwich. Jake sometimes brought a ten-cent package of Hostess chocolate cupcakes to school and traded each of them for half a sandwich.

Mom showed up, finally, smiling. "The check came! Sorry I'm late. I had to cash it. Here, you must be hungry." She handed me an egg. "Start with this."

I began peeling it and gooey egg white spilled out. The egg was raw.

"I'm not eating this!"

"It's fine. Opera singers eat raw eggs before every concert."

"I'm not an opera singer."

"If you're hungry it'll taste good."

"I want something normal to eat!" I shouted. "Can't you ever do anything normal?" I didn't mean to shout, but I had to get through to her.

Now Paul Kaplan was watching me. So was Laura Nusser and Julie Wolf. There was instant understanding between us: your mother is a crazy lady.

"Justine, don't raise your voice to me. Here, have some raisins."

I took the raisins.

"Nobody has any imagination," my mother said.

Chapter 4.

Closing In

Two years earlier, when I was eight, my brothers and I went to Surprise Lake Camp for three weeks. It was a nonprofit camp with a sliding scale, so it only cost seventy-five dollars for three weeks, and my father paid for it. I swam every day, learned folk dancing and sang in a musical about Hans Christian Andersen. On Friday nights we all wore white shirts and sat together on a hill overlooking the lake, singing Jewish songs during the brief Sabbath service.

I started writing a letter to my mother, but so much kept happening that I wanted to tell her about—the hike to the Mount Beacon funicular, a cable car that took us up the mountain; canoeing; toasting marshmallows over a campfire—and I didn't want to leave any of the excitement out of the letter so I put off sending it.

She wrote to Jake that I wasn't writing her and he gave me good advice. "Just send the letter."

I made her a leather wallet and put it in the envelope with the letter and put on four six-cent stamps. But it wasn't enough postage, so she didn't get the letter until October.

My mother was lonely in the city without me, so the following two summers she didn't let me go back to camp. Somehow, applications for my brothers were completed, but not for me.

We were staying in the Martinique Hotel on Thirty-Third Street the summer I was ten. I spent the sweltering days traipsing around Manhattan with her. We'd get up late, and she'd putter around with her papers. I'd be anxious to get out of the tepid hotel room and do something. Finally we might go over to Lamston's on Thirty-Fourth Street where she'd have coffee and an English muffin upstairs in the coffee shop, and I'd stand around the Classics comic book section reading *Lorna Doone, The Prince and the Pauper* or *Robinson Crusoe*.

We'd wander over to the United Nations so she could get one of the UN secretaries to give her a photo of Secretary General U Thant or Eleanor Roosevelt or Dag Hammarskjold for her book. Outside we'd stop at a deli on First Avenue and get two Kaiser rolls and a quarter pound of bologna, then go to the playground at the UN and make sandwiches with a plastic knife, sitting on the bench. Later we'd walk over to Crest's on Fifth Avenue to buy Band-Aids or antibiotic cream for her blisters, and look at stuff. I'd pick out a piece of pretty ribbon from a spool for ten cents to wear in my hair. Then we'd stop at the Doubleday Bookstore on Fifty-Fourth Street for an hour, where I read *Harriet the Spy.* I read it, just as I read *Little Women* and *The Secret Garden* and *The Princess and Curdie*, in increments of an hour, whenever we got to a bookstore. I read slowly, to savor every word. These were the little oases, the precious hours that broke up the loneliness of the summer days and weeks drifting around midtown, without friends or neighbors, without goals to achieve or purposeful activities. Nights we'd head back to the hotel. She'd boil some rice and *pupiklekh* (gizzards) for dinner on a hot plate. If we had a quarter to spare we'd watch TV for an hour. The TV had a little box with a slot that took quarters.

Every Monday we trudged across the bleakness of Thirty-Fourth Street to the General Post Office on Eighth Avenue for the support check. If it didn't come, we'd go back on Tuesday, sometimes Wednesday. I couldn't wait for school to begin in September.

When we had money from the check we'd sometimes drop into heaven for a few hours—an air-conditioned movie. The blast of cold air would save me, lift me into a more privileged world. After the movie we'd stop at Howard Johnson's on Sixth Avenue and Forty-Ninth Street, where there are cliffs of skyscrapers now. Back then Sixth Avenue was lined with lower, dark, seedy buildings, but Howard Johnson's was a haven of bright orange, teal and lemon upholstered banquettes filled with happy tourists. I'd spin around on a high stool at the counter and order a green pistachio ice cream cone. For half an hour I'd feel equal to the tourists.

In August we ran out of panties for me and had no money to buy new ones. Mom went to the home of a woman she had met at the playground and asked for a pair of her daughter's panties. Another time I had nothing to wear so I had to put on my mother's green sleeveless blouse, which was like a dress on me, with one of her belts around the waist to cinch it in. We took a subway train up to Washington Heights to get some money from her brother, my Uncle Sam.

The boys came back from camp in late August. School resumed. In September we left the Hotel Martinique because our bill had gotten out of hand, and the four of us spent another long night, trudging the streets.

One afternoon Mrs. Kushner put different denominator division problems on the blackboard, and we copied them into our notebooks to work out. After I finished mine I rested my head on the desk and closed my eyes.

"Are you sick?" I opened my eyes and saw my best enemy, Laura Nusser, looking at me with curiosity from her seat in the next aisle.

"No," I said. "Just tired."

Laura was thin and liked to suck on strands of her wispy, tangled, long blonde hair. We argued a lot.

"What time did you go to bed?"

"Eleven," I lied. "My older brother—the one in *college*—he stays up late, reading."

"Did you watch *The Ed Sullivan Show* last night?" asked Larry Kelly, a pale, chubby kid who was always talking about his grandfather, the comedian Henny Youngman. "He only gave my grandpa two minutes." Larry shook his head. "Why do Jewish divorces cost so much? They're worth it. Take my wife—"

"Please!" Laura and I yelled.

Laura stood up, lifted her dress and pulled her tights higher. She couldn't help it that she was so skinny her tights were always slipping down, but lifting her dress in front of half the class was the kind of annoying thing she did.

Although I had changed schools several times, she had moved along with me once, to a program for intellectually gifted children, so we'd been together for four years.

Mrs. Kushner came over.

"Are you all right?" she asked me.

"Yeah."

"You were squinting to see the blackboard before. Maybe you need glasses."

"I just need a good night's sleep."

"Why couldn't you sleep last night?"

I shrugged.

"Her brother's in college," Laura piped in. "He keeps the light on to read."

Mrs. Kushner wasn't convinced. "I want to have a talk with your mother."

During gym I perked up because we were learning square dancing.

"It's Sadie Hawkins Day," the gym teacher said. "Girls get to pick out a boy to dance with."

Laura, Valerie, Belinda, Gloria, a horde of girls swarmed around Paul Kaplan to be his partner. In his crisp white shirt and tie, he was excellent husband material and even a prepubescent girl could tell. He looked flattered, amused, perplexed; which girl to choose? I wanted him, and I thrust my hand through the gaggle of girls, grabbed Paul's hand and pulled him out. He was mine.

When my mother picked me up after school, Mrs. Kushner was waiting for her. The three of us went to the lunchroom and sat down at a long table with benches.

"I'm a little concerned about Justine. She has to squint to see the writing on the blackboard. Maybe she should have an eye checkup."

"Thanks. I don't think she needs glasses but I'll be aware of it."

"I'll go to bed early tonight," I offered.

"Justine is also late to school all the time and frequently absent. And she seems worried a lot. Is there anything going on that I should know about?"

"Is that a crime, to worry? There's a lot to worry about in life. It's not a good idea to pretend otherwise."

Mrs. Kushner was taken aback, but she got her bearings. "Your address is listed as the General Post Office."

"Mm-hm. We can be contacted there."

"Mrs. Blau, where are you living now? We need to know. It's the law."

My mother hesitated. "We're temporarily staying at a hotel in midtown while we wait for our next apartment to be ready."

"What hotel?"

My mother couldn't answer because we didn't have a new hotel yet. She stood up. "Justine will give you the exact address tomorrow. And now we'll be going."

Mrs. Kushner stood up too.

"Mrs. Blau, let me know if there's anything I can do to help."

I thought to myself, could Mrs. Kushner rescue us? Would she be the one to understand the situation and figure out what to do?

Mrs. Kushner continued. "I know you're raising three children alone. Do you get support from the children's father, or family, friends?"

"No. My parents are gone."

"My father sends a check every week." I piped in, trying to be upbeat.

"Well, if the child support isn't enough, there are social services agencies, welfare—"

My mother shook her head contemptuously. "That's not for people like us," she said, and we walked out.

After school Mom and I went to Horn & Hardart on Fifty-Seventh Street between Sixth and Seventh Avenues. We took a table in the balcony where it was less crowded. Mom gave me twenty cents and I went downstairs to the wall of little glass boxes with doors. I put in a dime, like a game, turned the silver handle and took out a sugared doughnut. I got my mother a cup of coffee in a white ceramic cup for ten cents. Then I filled a glass with water and took a straw and lemon slices, and at our table upstairs I poured sugar into my glass; free lemonade.

Nobody bothered us up in the balcony. After a while Leo came and sat at the table next to ours to spread out and do his homework. We had arranged to meet here, because we didn't know yet where we were staying that night. Now we had to wait for Jake who was at his after-school messenger job.

Leo became immersed in reading a play for his English class, *Who's Afraid of Virginia Woolf.* I went downstairs and got him a roll and butter and made him some lemonade. When I brought it to him he smiled, which lit up his face and showed his white, even teeth.

Without a book to read—we'd lost our rights to take out books from the public library long ago because we owed fines—I was bored. Through the balcony railing I peered down at a lady drinking hot chocolate below us. On impulse I crumpled the paper covering from my lemonade straw and made a spitball. As the lady below searched in her bag for something, I threw the spitball and it landed right in her cup. She jerked back from the splash and looked up, but I leaned back and she didn't see me. She just took the spitball out with a spoon, and I thought I had gotten away with it. But Jake was looking at me. He had just walked in and saw what happened as he came upstairs.

He was frowning. He put his books and stuff down at the table where Leo was sitting.

"Come here," he whispered. I sat down at their table. "That wasn't a nice thing to do, shrimp." I noticed the paper clip that kept his eyeglass frame together.

His uncharacteristic gentleness made me feel guilty.

"I know. But sometimes I feel like what difference does it make what I do? Even if we ever do get an apartment, it wouldn't be like a...a real apartment, would it?" Leo looked up as I spoke. "We'll never be normal," I continued. "Wherever we live it will be crazy."

"Yeah, but if we had an apartment with the rent paid, you could go to the same school every year," said Jake. "And make friends in the neighborhood. When you get older you could babysit."

Babysit.

"Jake, don't get her hopes up," Leo said.

Jake's nose was always red, but now it got redder.

"Oh, then you don't really believe Mom will work everything out?"

Leo looked quickly at Mom, but she was reading the newspaper, not listening to us.

"I don't believe everything Mom says. It's just that I think we should cooperate with her. Anyway, what else can we do?"

"Let's call Dad," said Jake.

"Dad?! Don't be stupid, Jake. Dad's not going to do anything to help us until we start seeing him again on Sundays—on his terms."

"He'd see us tomorrow, if Mom would let us go places with him in the car."

"Jake, let's face it. If he really wanted to see us, it wouldn't matter if we went in the car or not."

"That's true, Jake," I said.

"That's extortion!" Jake's face contorted, and a touch of saliva spewed out as he shouted. "How would you like it if your ex-wife wouldn't let you see your own kids unless you sold your car?"

Mom looked at us. "What are you talking about over there?"

Leo whispered. "Maybe Mom has a point." Leo's black eyebrows furrowed angrily, and his forehead wrinkled. "Maybe Dad should sell the car and give us the money. If he cares about us, he should do something!"

Every time one of my brothers spoke, I thought each made a good point.

Jake pointed his finger in Leo's face. "He's never going to sell that car, when she tries to force him into it."

Leo banged his fist on the table. "What's worth more to him—seeing us or keeping his car? It's been eight months since we've seen him."

"Maybe he'd be more generous if she was a little nicer," said Jake.

"Great. So he punishes us to prove his point?"

"Stop it. Stop it," I said.

The boys looked at each other.

Jake lowered his voice, pleading. "Look, Leo, let's call Dad already."

There was a public phone booth downstairs, and we went down together. Mom didn't really notice what we were doing.

It was Jake's idea, so he dialed the phone while Leo and I huddled around him. Jake nervously ran his fingers through his hair. His brown eyes behind his thick glasses looked melty.

As the phone rang, I pictured my father reading the paper in his neat apartment, while Gisela would be sitting with her feet up reading a fashion magazine. Her sons in Boy Scout uniforms are in their rooms, doing homework. Or playing basketball outside in the playground.

"Dad, it's Jake. We're having a hard time."

"I know you, Jake. Where are you staying now?"

"Dad, we've been moving around a lot. That's why I called. Can you help us get an apartment? What if you got an apartment and paid the rent directly? You know, you could deduct the rent from the child support check and just send Mom the rest. So the rent always got paid."

"Jakey boy, I'm sorry. Mom is too unstable. It just wouldn't work. After all these years, I know. She's too impossible. I'm so sorry you have to suffer because of her problems."

Jake answered desperately. "What about *us,* Dad?"

"I haven't forgotten about you," Dad said. "Help is on the way."

"What do you mean?"

"You'll see. I'm doing what I can."

At this point I grabbed the phone. "Daddy, aren't you going to help us?"

I heard my father fighting back tears. "Justine, I feel badly. I wish you and Leo and Jake could come live with Gisela and me. But your mother would fight that tooth and nail."

"But she's not taking care of us. Just because we don't live with you doesn't mean you can't still help us."

"Justine, Justine. Some people are going to talk to you," he said. "Social workers. They're going to try to help."

Words left me.

"Justine? Can you hear me?"

I hung up the phone and then realized I hadn't said goodbye.

Chapter 5

Resistance

Rush hour was subsiding and the RR train wasn't too crowded as we hauled our stuff—shopping bags, schoolbooks, Leo's guitar—onto the subway car down to Thirty-Fourth Street. Now that we had money from Dad's child support check, we could move back into a hotel.

The Wolcott Hotel on Thirty-First Street just west of Fifth Avenue was within our price range, meaning too expensive at forty dollars a week, but we could pay the first week's rent and hope it would work out—that somehow, miraculously, we'd get more money.

After climbing up the subway station steps with our bags, we walked down to Thirty-First and made a left at Broadway toward Fifth Avenue. The sidewalks were covered with more cigarette butts, black flattened gum spots, spit and garbage than our usual neighborhood around Central Park. The Empire State Building loomed over us, but it didn't do us any good because there were no trees or other kids around. This area was for businesses, not people. The buildings were gray slabs with grimy windows that hadn't been cleaned forever. I saw dirty exhaust pipes, filthy grates, a crummy deli with a neon Budweiser sign and stacks of Kools piled in the window. I wished we could go back to a neighborhood with families, a playground, dogs.

Leo walked ahead of us, brooding, unfocused. I took his hand, trying to make him feel better. Jake, I could tell, was plotting how to get rich, thinking about the stock market and investments; he'd show Dad. I thought, "Please God help us, please God help us, please God help us." Mom didn't know that we had called Dad, that he'd let us down, that we knew she was right about him, that he was a weak coward. But she had money in her pocket, and she began softly singing one of the songs she'd made up:

Love is a mutual affair.
A feeling two people may share.
I want you, need you, love you.
But you must want, love and need me too.

She kept looking at us, smiling. "C'mon, kids."

Her singing soothed me, but was annoying at the same time. Jake sneered at the idea of singing with her, Leo barely bothered to shake his head. I had to help her, so I joined in.

Tell me what I want to know.
What feelings for you may I show?
I want you, need you, love you,
'Cause love is a mutual affa-a-air.
That only a two-some may share.

Mom rewarded me with a kiss on my cheek. "That's my girl. *Shana madela.*"

We followed Mom up the marble steps, across the dirty flowered carpeting, and into the Wolcott lobby. While she checked us into the hotel I took in the dust-covered chandeliers, the chipped gold angels over the elevators, the old gent on the couch smoking a Kent—it was unbearably drab.

But upstairs our new hotel setup was okay—we had two rooms and our own bathroom.

"We're moving up in the world," Jake said, as he dropped his shopping bag down on one of the twin beds in the smaller room. "My bed." Leo glared at him, not sure if Jake got the best bed or not, but he let it go. Mom and I would share the queen-size bed in the bigger room, facing the street.

The all-white bathroom had an old-fashioned tub with feet, and there were enough towels for each of us. I had my first shower in many days, and I brushed my teeth in the elegant marble sink, a clean girl, as good as anyone else, happy to be with my brothers again, in our own place.

Leo strummed his guitar, and when I heard the chords to *The Cat Came Back,* from Surprise Lake Camp, I went in the boys' room. Jake, wearing a towel around his waist, was putting his clothes neatly in the chest of drawers, as he sang with Leo:

Old Mister Johnson had troubles of his own
He had a yellow cat which wouldn't leave its home

I joined in with them, jumping from Jake's bed to Leo's, back and forth.

He tried and he tried to give the cat away,
He gave it to a man goin' far, far away

Mom came in. "Now this is what I like to see. This does my heart good."

Jake mocked her. "Yes, let's enjoy our nice peaceful hotel room—until the next time we get kicked out."

"Don't start," Mom said. "Let's have a nice evening. Don't be a *bulvan.*"

"Okay, okay. I won't." He patted the bed. "Sit here, Mom."

"Put some clothes on, first." She sat down on his bed while he dashed into the bathroom, changed into pajamas, and came back out.

"Okay, we've given them forty bucks for the week, Mom." Jake leaned forward as he spoke gently to her, sitting across from her on Leo's bed. "So, that leaves only fifteen left from the check. Leo and I will chip in. I'm making a buck twenty-five at my messenger job, and I can probably put in ten a week. Leo, you're gonna find another job, right?"

"Yeah, yeah," Leo nodded.

"Still, Mom, we could use some more money coming in."

Mom sighed.

Jake took a creased copy of *The Times* out of a shopping bag. "I just want to talk about you getting a job." He went through the pages until he found the classified section. "Let's see if there's a job for you in the help wanted ads."

"Jakey boy, if it will make you happy, I'll do it."

They looked at the ads while Leo played a few chords from Dylan's "Blowin' In the Wind."

"Well, here's a fashion company," said Jake, reading. "They want a 'hardworking gal Friday. Gorgeous showroom, assist the owner, handle the phones.' They need someone who can type forty words per minute." Jake looked at her. "Would you consider learning to type?"

Mom giddily ignored him.

"Okay, here's a good one. 'Management trainees with excellent communication skills wanted.'" She looked up. "I certainly come in top of the class in that category, wouldn't you say, Justine?"

"Sure, Mom."

Mom continued looking at the ad. "Oh, I knew it. They're located in Brooklyn. I'm not going all the way down there. There's always a catch. You can't say I didn't try."

She put the paper down. Leo switched to playing *Ramblin' Rose*.

Jake practically snarled. "Other people manage to commute to work."

"Yeah, and other people become alcoholics and smoke. You have to find a balance in things." She smiled at her wisdom.

"Tell you what, lady," Jake stood up. "Just let us live in one steady apartment for a few years, and you can smoke and drink all the hell you want."

"Well, I do like to eat. Jakey, go down to that deli and bring back a snack."

Jake bought a small box of instant lemon pudding and a quart of milk. He mixed them together and let it thicken for a few minutes. Then he spooned it out into the glasses in the bathroom, and we took turns sharing the two spoons.

It was while we were at the Wolcott that I lost my faith in Judaism. It began with my fourth-grade play about King Arthur at PS 111. The biggest role was Merlin the Magician. Jake coached me for it, teaching me to deliver my lines in an authoritative voice and commanding manner. It was the deep voice that clinched it for me, and I won the part, beating out three boys.

I was learning my lines at home one day, shouting "Long live the King" and falling on one knee in front of the mirror. In the script everyone kneels to King Arthur at the end.

"Jews don't kneel before anyone but God," Mom said.

"Mom, it's just a play."

"It's against our religion to kneel."

"It's not real life. It's pretend."

"Symbolism is very important."

I wracked my brain to respond. "Jewish actors must kneel sometimes." I went through the list of Jewish actors I could think of: Danny Kaye, Paul Newman (half Jewish), Eddie Cantor, Tony Curtis. Kirk Douglas—did he kneel in *Spartacus?*

Finally Mom insisted that I tell the teacher, Miss Yalowitz, that I couldn't kneel, but I could bow instead.

Miss Yalowitz had the class vote on whether or not it would be okay if I just bowed, and I won—I could just bow—by one vote. But then the other Jewish kid in the show, Geoffrey Wolf, raised his hand.

"I'm Jewish too. If Justine can't kneel, then I can't either."

"That's it. I can't make exceptions," said Miss Yalowitz. "Justine you're not doing Merlin anymore. Juan, you take over the part."

I had *believed* in Miss Yalowitz. She knew my mother was difficult; she knew we didn't have much money. I thought she was on my side.

After school, Laura Nusser and I walked up Fifty-Second Street. "You're a good Jew," she said, and in that moment I thought, *If Judaism takes this role away, then I don't think I want to be Jewish.* But I knew it was my mother who used Judaism to take this role away from me.

Mom pulled this stunt on Jake, too. He was chosen with two other kids from Brandeis High School on West Eighty-Fourth Street to be on the TV show *It's Academic.* Mom found out the show was taped on a Saturday and nixed it.

"It's Shabbos, you can't do it."

"Oh, I'm going, lady."

Mom's rules about Jewish rituals were flexible when she wanted them to be. We weren't allowed to write on the Sabbath, but we ate shrimp and lobster at Chinese restaurants.

The morning of the taping, Jake ironed his white shirt on the bed and slicked his hair back with Brylcreem while Mom yelled.

"Don't you dare go." She paced nervously, throwing out brochures and papers, rinsing some cups in the bathroom sink, moving from one thing to another, aggravated. As Jake started leaving, she hit him with a shoe. He lifted his arm to fend her off and ran outside. She opened the window of our room and when he appeared on the street, yelled out.

"Jake! Come back!"

But he kept going. I didn't understand how Jake got the courage to disobey her. His team came in third, but the prize for the third-place team was a new set of *Encyclopedia Britannica* for the high school library, and the school librarian told Jake that a new encyclopedia was just what the school needed.

Mom waited until the Christmas sales to get me a winter coat. That winter of 1966 Jake walked around in a thin cotton jacket from Alexander's department store, and had a cough that lasted for months. If Mom had let us see Dad, he would have gotten Jake a coat.

One day after school Jake and I were at a pizza place having a slice and a cup of water. After a while one of the pizza guys brought two grape drinks to us.

"These are for you. Guy just paid for these drinks."

"Who?"

"He left. He wanted you to have it."

Jake and I looked at each other, thrilled. It gave us the feeling that people could look out for us.

Chapter 6.

The Summons

One night in June Mom decided we needed to leave the Wolcott.

"Let's go," she said.

Jake stood up, immediately yelling. "But the rent is paid!"

"We're going," she insisted.

"No, this is crazy. Who's staying with me? Leo?"

Leo was on the fence. Jake looked at me. He could usually count on me to be on his side.

"Justine, let's stay." I knew that I could not let my mother down. She needed me, and I had to be by her side. And if I had to be with her, I wanted Jake and Leo with me. I didn't want to be alone with her. "We should do what Mom says."

"I can't believe this," Jake said. The four of us checked out of the hotel and when we got outside, Mom said to the boys, "Find a place to stay." They were on their own. I had been duped, and now Jake was mad at me.

Jake spent the night at Kenny's, and Leo spent the night at a friend's house too. The next day they called our father and he set them up in a double room at the Thirty-Fourth Street YMCA. I never went to my brothers' room at the YMCA—women weren't allowed in the men's section. I imagined a room with two twin beds on metal frames. Jake would be lying on one, throwing his baseball up in the air and catching it over and over. Leo would have his college English books. They'd have a transistor radio, and Jake would listen to baseball games on 1010 WINS. They'd have some food staples, just like we used to have. Wonder bread and margarine on the windowsill. Leo's guitar, in its frayed black cardboard case, would be in a corner.

In September, after working at camp, Leo got a tiny apartment on East Fifth Street between First and Second Avenue for sixty dollars a month, and Jake went off to S.U.N.Y. Stonybrook.

And that was it. I had no idea that the four of us would never live together again.

Mom and I stayed for awhile in a room at the Allerton Hotel on Fifty-Seventh Street and Lexington Avenue. It was near my fifth-grade class at PS 59 and only cost ten bucks a night.

PS 59 was a very good public school in Sutton Place, so some wealthy kids went there for elementary school, before later going on to private school in seventh grade. I'd go play at their homes after school, and then have to go back to our hotel room with Mom.

My father took me to Macy's one day after school and bought me white rubber over-boots and a pair of good brown loafers. Soon after, I went to my friend's house, and she told her mother, "Look Mom, Justine has new shoes."

My favorite friend in fifth grade was Stephanie Brooks, Mel Brooks's daughter. She told me in hushed tones about the movie he was working on, *Springtime for Hitler*, later changed to *The Producers*. One day after school she and I walked to the Donnell Library, and we passed him on the street. (Her parents were divorced.) "Hello,

Stephanie," he said, patting her head. He stopped momentarily, was distantly amused to hear she was going to the library, and walked on.

One night Mom and I had no place to sleep, so she looked up her favorite English teacher from decades ago at Washington Irving High School. The lady lived in a one-bedroom apartment in the Amalgamated co-ops on Ninth Avenue in the Twenties. We slept on her convertible couch for a few nights.

During the winter Mom got a terrible cold and was depressed while we were staying at the Martha Washington Hotel on West Twenty-Ninth Street. She let me go to the deli down the block a few times for chicken soup and tuna sandwiches, but mostly I stuck with her in the hotel room. Luckily I had a school library book with me, *Ishi,* about the last surviving member of the Yahi tribe of American Indians. Poor Ishi, so lonely without his people.

The court had arranged that my father would see me on Sundays. Family court document [April 20, 1967] reports:

```
All children seem devoted to mother
and not interested in father. Jus-
tine is bright but defies authority.
Is defiant generally. Mother was told
she'd be held in contempt if she
wasn't quiet. Visitation privileges
by father established, Sundays 10
a.m. to 5 p.m.
```

One Sunday Dad drove me to his apartment in Stuyvesant Town, a housing complex from Fourteenth Street to Twentieth Street east of First Avenue. He insisted I get in his car, the car my mother had forbidden us to ride in. I was his daughter, he explained, and I was going to ride in his car. He didn't seem connected to me as he drove, just determined that he wasn't going to let my mother decide how he and I would spend our time together. All the red brick buildings of Stuyvesant Town looked alike. When we walked into the bright apartment a teenage boy, one of my father's stepsons, was vacuuming. He smiled kindly to me, pitying me, the unlucky child visiting normal people. We had lunch, salami sandwiches and potato salad, at the kitchen table with Gisela and her four sons. Their living room was orderly; an original painting by Chaim Gross and a profile of Gisela's Austrian Jewish mother hung over the olive green couch; the credenza was topped with dozens of her sons' sports trophies and a plaque honoring my father for being den father to his stepsons' Boy Scout troop.

That visit Dad gave me roller skates for my birthday. And as I left, Gisela gave me a Sara Lee cake to take home with me. Dad brought me back to the brownstone where Mom and I were staying, but she wasn't there. So Dad left me at a playground in Central Park. When I found Mom later, she was livid that Dad had introduced me to Gisela and had brought me to their apartment. She threw out the Sara Lee cake, and we promptly took the subway trip back to his building, where we left the roller skates outside his apartment door.

Afterwards, we sat on a bench as Mom brooded.

"They're gonna get it. But good."

"Mom, we have to meet the boys. Let's go."

"Yeah, yeah. Soon." I didn't know what was going on except for a sense of hopelessness. Mom had picked up a *Reader's Digest* and I read a story about a handyman in an elementary school who had a seemingly magic way of dealing with children.

Gisela worked for Fruit of the Loom, on Fiftieth Street and Sixth Avenue, not far from the Donnell Library. As luck would have it, my mother bumped into her a few days later.

As she told it, and as I imagine it, my mother gazed intently at Gisela walking briskly in her stilettos. My mother would have been a volcano, Gisela oblivious. With her businesslike dress, pearls and severe short hair, Gisela was a perfectly put together victim-to-be.

My mother went up to her. "What's your name?"

"Gisela Blau."

"You rotten homebreaker!"

Gisela stopped, horrified.

"My kids have no place to live, and it's all your fault."

"Excuse me." Gisela tried to retreat.

"Take this, you lousy bitch! You *f'shtinkener pishka!*" Gisela tried to make a run for it, but my mother swung her large purse and whacked it across Gisela's head. Gisela stumbled and almost fell down, dropping her purse. Blood ran down Gisela's cheek from her eye. Gisela, a terrified, spindly Chihuahua, grabbed her purse and ran down into the subway.

Mom told me what she'd done after she picked me up from school.

"Mom, why did you do that?"

"I didn't like the way she said 'Gisela Blau.' Anyway, I didn't take a knife to her. She deserved it. I gave her a *schmeiss.* She got a crack on the head." I was humiliated that my mother hit Gisela; but there was a smidgen, an undercurrent of a thrill, that Mom had the guts to take some revenge on Dad's Concubine, who had taken our place while we were neglected. The family court document [May 2, 1967] reports:

Mr. Blau said that Mrs. Blau is dangerous. April 28, 1967 she accosted his present wife at subway entrance 6th Avenue and 50th Street and slapped her across the face causing a hemorrhage of the eye. Mrs. Blau has been getting $25 a week for Justine and sons each get $15 each which Mr. Blau says they give to their mother. She keeps moving because she cannot pay the rent.

Possible need of emergency placement.

That slap reverberated in my life for years afterward. It cost me.

The next night we stopped at Leo's apartment to see him, but as we approached, he happened to come outside, and he was with a beautiful, tall and slender black girl.

My mother flipped into another dimension. *"Schwarza,"* she snarled, spitting at the ground. Leo saw her, hesitated, put his arm around his girlfriend and walked very quickly away.

That night my mother and I walked through the city, and she spit in front of numerous black people that we passed. Two black people, outraged by her spitting, were going to retaliate, but I looked at them imploringly, and in those two to three seconds they got it that this was mental illness more than hate, and because I was there they just stopped and let her alone.

On my eleventh birthday my mother tried to pass off "birthday soup" in place of birthday cake at Chock full o'Nuts. I said 'fuck you, lady' for the first time, and she slapped me.

The family court document [May 9, 1967] reports:
Mrs. Blau came to court this
morning, son, Leo and Justine were

with her....She is presently living
at the Martinique Hotel (33rd St)
and is hoping for an apartment with
a kitchen on Thursday. Judge told
her that she should inform the
Court if she gets it. He adjourned
the case until June 6th. Warned her
that she should follow through as
to the order of protection as far
as visitation is concerned. If she
does not follow through, the case
should be advanced. Also ordered
her to have Justine return to
school....I understand that before we
went into Court, there was quite a
scene between Mrs. Blau and Miss
DeValera.

[May 24, 1967]
Spoke to Mrs. Pearl Mayer (Jewish Family Services worker at 22nd
St). Said that Mrs. Blau came to
see her 5/17/67 in need of carfare
and lunch money. Spoke of her need
for help and said that if she had
sufficient money she would have no
problems."

[May 26, 1967]
Mrs. Blau not complying with court
order on father's visitation. She
is due in court with an attorney
on 6/9…He said Mrs. Blau threatened to leave New York with Justine
if she does not get her own way.

[June 5, 1967]
Leo and Jake Blau, Justine's brothers, came in to speak with us.
Since the case is on to-morrow,
they were concerned about what may
happen. I was impressed with both
these boys. They feel that the
mother's condition is getting worse
and they can readily understand
the reason why Justine should be
placed. Wanted to know about the
kinds of placement and I explained
to them what the procedures would
be if the Court ordered placement.
Jake is home from Stony Brook College and will be going to Surprise
Lake Camp to work as a counselor
later in the month. Leo, who is
in his last year in City College,
has taken an apartment at 331 East

5th Street. Jake is staying with
him now. We talked about the pos-
sibility of Justine staying with
them until she can be prepared for
placement and they thought that
Justine might accept this.

[June 6, 1967]
Mr. Blau, attorney, Guidance Counselor, SPCC [Society for the Pre-
vention of Cruelty to Children]
Worker and Justine's brothers in
Court. Mrs. Blau and Justine were
not there, but about Noon boys
went downstairs and apparently
Justine and mother drove up in a
cab. Boys paid for cab, and after
some conversation with mother gave
her some money and she left with
Justine, never appearing for court
hearing. Accordingly Judge pro-
ceeded without her, made a finding, issued warrant for Justine to
be brought in and for emergency
placement by JBC [Jewish Board of
Guardians].

On June 7th I was called to the school office where I was led into a room to be interviewed by Mr. Lipschitz, a Children's Aid Society social worker.

He sat opposite me, smiling coldly. "I understand that you're a great reader."

"Yeah."

"Your father said that you slept in Central Park recently. Has that happened more than once?"

"Oh, no," I said. "We were just a little short of money that night. These things happen."

He nodded. "That must have been hard for you, though."

I shrugged.

"Where are you staying now, Justine?

"At the Martha Washington Hotel on Twenty-Ninth Street."

He made a note. "How many rooms do you have there?"

"One."

"Did you have breakfast this morning?"

"Oh, yes! I had an English muffin at Bickford's."

"I see. Good. And is there any food in the hotel room? A refrigerator or hot plate?"

"We're only there temporarily. In the meantime, we feel that Bickford's serves a nice, wholesome breakfast."

"How do you feel about your mother, Justine?"

"Are you using psychology on me?"

He made a note. "Not really. It's just that you were absent from school forty days last year, and you were late over sixty times. You come to school looking as if you haven't slept, and you don't have adequate clothes. And your family moves around like Gypsies. We're concerned about you."

I was caught off guard. That was a lot of days to be absent and late. I was just living through each day, and didn't realize how the latenesses added up. And I never wanted to miss school. It just happened.

"Well, uh, we would like to get an apartment. Do you know of any? They're hard to find."

"You're very loyal to your mother, aren't you?"

I shrugged.

"Is your mother picking you up after school?"

I nodded.

"Well, here's something very important I want you to give her."

He handed me an envelope.

As soon as I reached the stairwell I sat down on a step and carefully opened the envelope. It read:

```
Mrs. Martha Blau,
You are hereby summoned to appear
at Family Court at 301 West 23rd
Street, NY NY on May 22nd, 1967 at
10 a.m.
Social Services against Mrs. Martha
Blau, case #57432
```

My hands shook as I folded the summons up, and I dropped the envelope three times before I could put the summons back in. I stayed in the stairwell a few minutes, not sure what to do with myself, scratching the skin of my chest with my nails. What was Mom doing today? I didn't know. Why didn't she get a job? What should I have said to that man? I should get back to class but I wanted to stay here in the staircase for a while. What did the summons mean? What would happen? I stood up. I sat down. Would Mom give me 20 cents to get French fries at the coffee shop after school? Eventually I went back to my classroom.

My mother was late after school. Finally I could see her big pale yellow cloth hat from a distance. She walked slowly toward me, limping from her blisters. We kissed on the cheek.

"A social worker came for me today, Mr. Lipschitz."

"What?!"

"I think he was from the Children's Aid Society."

"It's the stinker. He put them up to it. What did you tell him?"

She handed me half a Mr. Goody bar. I took a bite.

"I told him we were between apartments."

"Good. What did he ask you?"

"He wanted to know where we were staying, if we had a kitchen, what we ate for breakfast."

Mom and I walked east on Fifty-Seventh Street to use the bathroom at The Plaza. "That creep. I'm supposed to bring three kids up on the lousy fifty-five a week he sends? And now he sics the social workers on me."

A crowd of people was grouped around a limousine in front of The Plaza, and as we got closer we saw people jostling to get a man's autograph.

"John Glenn!" Mom was suddenly alert. I looked for an astronaut but after a while realized that even though he had circled the Earth in a rocket ship, today he was just one of the men wearing a regular suit. He was balding too, like my father, but even so, he looked powerful.

"Get his autograph!" Mom was rifling through her purse to find a piece of paper. "It'll be worth something."

"I can use my composition book." She nodded and I pushed through the people. I was the only kid so I could get away with it, and thrust my black and white marble notebook at him.

"Mr. Glenn, can I have your autograph?"

Up close I saw how bright his blue eyes were in his tanned face, how confident he was. Like from another world. He smiled down at me and signed my notebook.

I was in a daze the rest of that day. We went to Central Park. All I know is, I lost the notebook. I lost John Glenn's autograph, somewhere, just uptown from the playground. And in that book was the summons. So Mom didn't know there was a summons. And I forgot about it.

The next day I told everyone in my class that I met John Glenn and got his autograph.

"Where is it?"

"I lost it."

They didn't believe me.

Another day after school Mom and I browsed in FAO Schwartz, roaming past the life-sized log cabin and a motorized child-sized car.

I took her hand, inspecting her chipped nail polish.

"Grandpa used to tell this story," she said, "about a poor, very quiet man named Bontsche. Even though he was unlucky and lived in poverty all his life, this man never complained. So when he died he went straight to heaven; angels sang to him and God said to him, 'Bontsche, what do you want as your just reward?' And do you know what Bontsche asked for? 'All I'd like is a warm roll with fresh butter every morning,' said Bontsche."

Something about this story annoyed me. "Would it be so bad to ask God for nice things, after he'd been poor for so long?" I asked.

Mom put on an authoritative voice. "Bontsche was a truly pious man."

We stopped at a coffee shop on Fifty-Eighth Street and Fifth Avenue where there was a saying decoratively printed on the wall, which I had memorized:

"As you pass through life brother, whatever be your goal, keep your eye upon the doughnut, and not upon the hole."

Mom bought a chocolate glazed doughnut and broke it in two, handing me half.

We walked over to the Indian Tea Center on Fifty-Sixth Street between Fifth and Sixth Avenue, were we could get tea and graham crackers for free. We were not the kind of patrons they had in mind—they were hoping to publicize Indian tea—but we went there once a week anyway.

After that we went over to the Donnell Library. While Mom got engrossed in a magazine, I walked downstairs, went outside and, on impulse, headed for Temple Emanuel. I decided to steal a fur coat so we could sell it and use the money for an apartment.

Inside the synagogue lobby an elderly man wearing a yarmulke was stacking prayer books. The cloakroom was open and a few coats were hanging inside. I peeked in the sanctuary where a choir practiced singing a hymn accompanied by an organ. Wild with fear, I sat in the back row to assess the situation.

Now the elderly man ambled in carrying an armload of books, and started putting them in the slots in the backs of the pews. While he did that I slipped out and went straight for the cloakroom. Quickly I rifled through the coats. I found a fur coat, looked up to see if anyone was coming, and pulled it off its hanger. I folded it up and frantically searched for a bag. There was a shopping bag full of yarmulkes and I fumbled with it, turning it over to empty out the yarmulkes, and tried to stuff the fur coat into the bag. It didn't fit, so I turned the coat inside out, folded it up and started to leave with the coat under my arm. Then I looked up and the elderly man was staring at me.

"What are you doing?" he said, in a Yiddish accent.

"My…my mother left her coat here."

"Your mother left her coat? What's your name?"

"I have to go." If he understood my situation, he would let me keep the coat. I needed it more than whoever owned it. I started to leave, still holding on to the coat.

"No, no," he yelled. "Help! Rabbi! Help!

I dropped the coat and tried to get past the man. He grabbed me. We heard footsteps, and in desperation I bit his hand and he let go. I got past him but then the choirmaster grabbed the back of my shirt and held me.

When the police got there they asked me a lot of questions. I told them my father was a former policeman, and they asked where he worked, and they called him. I rode next to my father to the station house on Fiftieth Street between Third and Second Avenue.

"Justine, why on earth did you try to steal a fur coat?" he asked.

"So we could sell it and have money for an apartment. Dad, how could you do this to us? When I asked you to help us, I didn't think you'd take Mom to court."

He stroked my back, in methodical, short strokes. I wasn't used to anyone stroking my back. I wasn't sure how I felt about it. On the one hand he was taking my mother to court on a charge of negligence, but he was trying to reassure me.

When I was little and saw my father on Sundays, I liked to walk with him holding hands. I'd fold my hand into a fist and he'd wrap his big hand securely around mine.

They sent someone to get my mother at the Donnell Library and brought her back to the police station.

The captain spoke to her. "Mrs. Blau, we'll let Justine go about the fur coat. The synagogue doesn't want to press charges. But there's been a warrant out for your arrest. It seems you never showed up for hearings at Family Court."

Mom called Leo with her one phone call.

"Leo, we have a crisis! They're taking Justine away from me! Your father instigated the whole thing. *He's* the one who should be taken away! He's the one! We're at the police station. Call the newspapers! He can't get away with this. Tell the *Times*, call the *Post*."

My father paced while she was on the phone. Then he sat next to me.

"Justine, I couldn't let things go on as they were. Going to Family Court may help get the situation under control."

He was so gray, his whiskers sharp, not healthy, not attractive. "I'm sorry Justine. This isn't what I had in mind for you ever. I wanted a good life for you. I still do."

When my mother got off the phone and saw me with my father, she gestured to me to get away from him.

"Justine!" I went and stood beside her. The captain came over to us.

"Mrs. Blau, I've been in touch with the Child Welfare Bureau. Because you didn't show up, I have no choice but to hold you overnight and bring you to Family Court tomorrow. We're taking you downtown for the night. Your daughter can stay with her father and see you tomorrow at the Family Court hearing."

My mother clutched my hand. The captain continued. "I want to assure you that this is only a temporary situation, and you will be assigned to a lawyer first thing tomorrow morning."

She kept her tight grip on my hand, but restrained herself as she spoke, quietly using her best charm technique.

"Captain, there's no need for this. Please let me retain custody of my daughter, and you have my word I will be at court tomorrow with my daughter."

"Sorry, ma'am."

I started to cry and Mom turned her back on my father and the captain, and hugged me. The captain nodded at a policeman who moved toward Mom.

"Don't touch me." She stood and glared at them.

I wanted her to go along with what they wanted and not make a scene. "Mommy."

"Let's go, Justine. We're getting out of here."

She turned to leave. I knew it was useless. "Mom, please." Another policeman moved toward us.

The policemen moved to take her. She swung her purse at the first policeman, getting him hard by the ear. He winced. Both policemen were astonished. They hadn't thought it would come to this, but they took out their handcuffs.

"Oh God!" she yelled.

My father moved toward me. "Justine, stand to the side."

"My heart, my heart!" my mother clutched at her chest. I didn't believe her, but I was distraught at the hysteria. She started to fall but they held her up. Her hat fell off.

"Mommy! Mommy!"

I picked up her hat. Two more policemen grabbed my mother.

"Don't touch me. Get off me." She tried to back away from them.

I yelled at them, "Leave her alone! Get off my mother!"

I tried to pry them off her but one of them pulled me away. They put handcuffs on her.

My father picked up my mother's purse, which had fallen during the melee. How weak he is, I thought, how passive.

The captain said to my father, "Bring your daughter to Family Court at nine o'clock a.m."

I had never expected to see my mother handcuffed and arrested, or that I would be taken away from her. Although I'd endured all kinds of hardships, in some ways I was naive. I didn't know about sex or how babies were conceived. I'd rarely been hit. It seemed to me we basically had enough to eat and we managed, even if sometimes we didn't know where the next meal was coming from.

I spent the night at Leo's tiny sixth-floor walk-up apartment on East Fifth Street. Jake had finished his first year of college and was staying at Leo's until his summer job as a dishwasher at Surprise Lake Camp started.

Leo's studio, facing south to the street, had an ancient bathtub, a small table and two wooden chairs in the main room, and a sleeping alcove in the back. There were cockroaches but it was comforting to be with my brothers again. Leo didn't have a couch yet, so we did the old removing of the box spring thing, and they shared the mattress and I slept on the box spring. As we got ready for bed, Leo strummed on his guitar and I asked Jake to tell another Chocolate man story.

He sat on a chair with his feet up on the table. Normally Leo would get annoyed at him for this, but he let it slide this time.

"Well, the last time we saw the Chocolate man, the rich man bit off part of his nose. So now the Chocolate man ran outside and slipped through the woods. He came to a house and snuck inside and stole some clothes to wear. He also stole just enough money to buy some Hershey's chocolate at the store. He made himself a wife. And he used very thick chocolate so she was bullet proof."

"Meantime, the rich man had a big wife and he made her a steel girdle. So now both men could hide behind their wives when they were attacked.

"The chocolate man and his wife moved into an abandoned factory. They began buying chocolate wholesale and started a family. They created a whole chocolate dynasty."

It was the last time the three of us ever spent a night together.

I scarcely thought about the idea of living with Leo. He was twenty, finishing up his college degree. Even though Dad was helping him pay the rent, I knew it was enough for Leo to be able to work, go to college, keep his apartment, and have a few friends, sometimes a girlfriend. It would be too much to have an eleven-year-old living with him. And, much as I loved him, it would have been lonely for me.

I didn't have a change of clothes on me, so the next morning I still wore my blue paisley miniskirt, a light blue button-down blouse with a Peter Pan collar, white wide belt, white knee socks and my brown worn-down loafers. My father took us out to breakfast at the Second Avenue Deli. I had pancakes and orange juice all to myself.

"Did you know that your mother smacked Gisela last month?" my father asked Jake and Leo.

"Yeah. Is Gisela all right?" Jake asked. Leo was silent.

"Gisela's face was swollen. She had a hemorrhage in her eye. We were going to ask to have Justine live with us, but now I can't jeopardize Gisela's safety."

"Who said I want to live with you anyway?" I blurted loudly.

My father looked at me sadly. "My first priority is to my wife. I'm sorry Justine."

Just like when someone is sleepwalking and can come into full consciousness in a second, in this case I switched from alertness into a vagueness. Something is wrong here.

The four of us went to Family Court on Twenty-Third Street and sat around the waiting room for hours. I read *The New York Times Book Review* and hoped that the guards noticed.

After awhile my "advocate," a young Jewish man with curly hair, not much older than Leo and Jake, came to the waiting room and brought me to his tiny office.

"Justine, this is the charge against your mother." He had a framed diploma from Queens College on the wall, and on his bulletin board was a scrap of paper with Sandy Koufax's autograph.

He came over to my side of the desk and read out loud:

```
Mrs. Blau has failed to maintain
a stable home for herself and her
daughter by constantly moving from
place to place and hotel to hotel.
Hotel rooms used for one-night
stands are not suitable places for
a child to grow.
```

The advocate looked up at me with a kindly expression for a second. I leaned forward. I had to show him I was smart, worthy of being rescued.

```
The child is frequently absent
from school. Child is often
unkempt. Child is adjudicated a
neglected child.
```

"Justine, do you understand what that means?"

He had a slight double chin, probably from eating Entenmann's cakes out of the box in his parents' two-bedroom apartment in Jackson Heights. My brothers were more handsome and muscular than he was.

"Well, sometimes I have dandruff. Maybe that's one of the reasons they want to take me away from my mother." I spoke quickly because I had to get through to him. "But it's because I don't like to take showers when we stay in hotels with bathrooms in the hall that other people use. Otherwise, I would take showers more."

"I have dandruff too." He smiled and seemed to understand. "Listen, I'm representing you. Is there anything you'd like me to tell the judge?"

"They shouldn't take me away from my mother. She didn't just keep me out of school. She takes me to the *United Nations*. We read in *bookstores*."

He nodded and took me back to the waiting room. I sat next to my brothers; I wanted that to last as long as possible.

A young mother brought her toddler to the bathroom to change his diaper, but when she came back, his little green pants were still around his ankles. She couldn't even manage to pull his pants up.

"She's high," my brother explained.

People watched her surreptitiously as her little boy kept crying. "Stop that baby shit," she said to him.

My father had been mostly quiet, but he spoke softly to me now.

"You know, Justine, there's a certain irony about your being here in Family Court. You were named after a Family Court judge."

He told me a story from when he was a policeman. Two juvenile delinquents with bruises on their faces, were brought before

Family Court Judge Justine Wise Polier. She got the kids to tell
her that the detectives had beaten them up to get their confessions.
Judge Polier sent for the detectives who had arrested the boys and
told them if they ever beat up kids again, she'd have them prosecuted
to the fullest extent of the law. My father said that the word spread
like lightning throughout the police precincts in the city that it was
no longer acceptable to beat up juvenile delinquents to get confessions out of them. It cut down on police brutality.

Soon I was reunited with my mother and sat with her. Around
four, the judge called all of us—my mother, brothers, and father—
into a hearing room, much smaller than the courtrooms on *Million
Dollar Movie* and *Perry Mason*. We sat at a long table in front of
the judge. I was next to my mother and Leo, then Jake, and my
father was at the end. A guard stood beside the judge. I gripped my
mother's yellow hat as the judge read from a family court document

```
[June 16, 1967]:
It has been affirmatively demon-
strated that Respondent Mother has
failed to maintain a stable home
for herself and her daughter by
constantly moving from place to
place and hotel to hotel. Hotel
rooms used for one-night stands
are not suitable places for a
child to grow. Child is adjudi-
cated a neglected child pursuant
to Section 312 of the Family Court
```

```
Act. Petitioner Father's failure
to provide more adequately for
the support of Respondent and her
three children may well have trig-
gered Respondent's ultimate behav-
ior in failing to provide a stable
home for her ten-year-old daugh-
ter. Nonetheless the court cannot
condone her action inasmuch as she
had custody of the child and was
obliged to seek out all the nec-
essary help for herself and her
child so that the child could be
properly cared for….Remand of child
to Pleasantville Cottage School.
Notify parties and counsel.
```

"Martha Blau, your daughter, Justine, will be made a ward of the court and temporarily be put into placement. But this isn't a final decision. If you get a job and an apartment, you can petition the court to regain custody. Do you understand?"

My mother ignored him, sneering at my father. "Happy now?" Her voice was deep. "You should drop *dead.*"

"Theoretically, you could have your daughter back in three weeks," the judge said.

The Pleasantville Cottage School is a 175-acre campus in Pleasantville, in Westchester County, an hour north of New York City, run by the Jewish Child Care Association.

My brothers escorted me to my new home. I was entering a new world, against my wishes, and they weren't going to be part of that world. My brothers and I hadn't lived together for a year, and mercifully I didn't know then that I would never even spend a night in the same place with Leo again, and scarcely with Jake.

The man who drove us wore a black suit and derby hat, and silently drove a big black car while smoking a cigar. Jake rolled the window down to wave the cigar smoke out. "This guy thinks he's in a Damon Runyon story."

"Or Dickens," Leo whispered, then glanced at me. "But Pleasantville won't be like a workhouse. I mean, *Oliver Twist* was a long time ago."

"I know," I reassured him.

"They'll let you have seconds on gruel, no problem." Jake smiled, and I leaned back, inhaling their big brother smells, still safe between them in the back seat. We passed from Manhattan into the Bronx, miles of midsize buildings, pairs of underwear drying on laundry lines tied to fire escapes, a dilapidated Associated Food Mart, a Puerto Rican lady leaning on a pillow half out the window, salsa music in the humid air.

Social workers had visited me at school, and I saw the court summons my mother got, but it had never dawned on me that my mother would be handcuffed and arrested, and that I would be taken away from her.

After awhile the world became greener: private homes surrounded by trees, swing sets, swimming pools, a dog in a yard, more trees.

Several months earlier, while waiting around for my mother in the United Nations bookstore, I'd read a book about a Lebanese boy who became a refugee and was sent to an orphanage where the kids slept in a long barracks with rows of beds on each side. He was glad to get his own toothbrush. I pictured Pleasantville as being like that.

The car took us past signs for Yonkers, Valhalla, Briarcliff. I realized I had forgotten to give my mother back her hat.

After about an hour we turned right up a long road lined with huge beautiful oak trees, passing several large two-story beige cottages trimmed with white shutters. From the outside the cottages looked like something out of *The Sound of Music*, and the grounds were leafy and green. We came to a large square of lawn, almost the size of a city block. Straight ahead, beyond the square, was a four-story school building, framed on both sides by a colonnade (a covered walkway with huge white columns). Around the other sides of the square were more cottages.

"Could be worse," said Jake.

A boy walked stiffly on the grass, arms curved in front of him, as though on a steering wheel. "Forty-Second Street, Times Square!" the boy yelled, then stopped, in a trance. "Ding-dong! Watch the closing doors!" He started walking again. "Next stop Thirty-Fourth Street! Herald Square. Macy's." Again he lurched to a stop. Sweet-looking boy, black shiny hair, a robotic version of Jake.

"He's an IRT train," said Leo, solemnly shaking his head.

"Is he the train or the conductor?" Jake shook his head. "Whichever, I hope the kids aren't all like this."

Our car made a right and a left and stopped at the far corner of the square.

"Cottage 6," the driver said.

Cottage 6 had a large front porch facing the central square. To the right side of the house was a picnic table. I got out, putting on my mother's hat.

Inside, a Negro woman in her fifties, reddish hair pulled back in a bun, smiled at us behind granny glasses on a chain.

"Justine, I'm Lillie, one of your cottage parents." She took my hand in both of hers. "Welcome."

Jake extended his hand, returning the woman's smile, and without missing a beat gave her the *we're nice, genteel people* act, "Hi-i," he crooned. "I'm Jake, Justine's brother."

Leo was a college student, Jake was a sixteen-year-old high school senior—two nice, well-spoken boys with glasses, button-down shirts and chinos. Lillie was charmed by them.

Two girls clomped down the stairs. The short, red-headed girl had huge breasts and wore gobs of thick black eyeliner and mascara. As she came closer I saw big purple hickeys on her neck. Her bright hair curved under her heart-shaped chin and she was cute, but all I saw at that moment were the hickeys and the makeup. The other girl, big, sixteen years old going on forty, half hiding behind the long, dull strands of a brown wig, had wounded dog eyes, the most mournful eyes I had ever seen, outlined in the same thick eye makeup as her friend's.

Lillie introduced Crystal (breasts and hickeys) and Jody (wig). Leo and Jake were too stunned to speak. Jody lowered her head, murmuring a weak hello.

"Nice hat," Crystal sneered. I took the hat off.

Lillie clicked her fingernails sternly. "Crystal. Go down to the basement and get me some sheets for Justine."

"Lillie, we got things to do, people to see."

Lillie brushed up against Crystal, glowering at her fiercely. "You think you're a woman, girl?"

The girls drifted away. Jake lifted his fists and went into a boxer's stance. "Shrimp, anyone starts with you, remember, dukes up, cover your face."

I nodded.

"C'mon, Jake, don't scare her." Leo put his arm around me.

"We'll take good care of her," Lillie assured them. "It's true Justine will be the youngest girl in the cottage. The others are twelve to sixteen years old. But Justine's an emergency case, and this was the only cottage that had an opening."

Lillie moved toward the TV room, and we followed her. Several girls were watching *Dark Shadows.* Gina, wearing very thick glasses, form-fitting black-and-white checked pedal pushers and a patent leather belt, lay on the couch, her head in the lap of a fat girl, Brenda Silberstein. Simcha, a freckle-faced girl with kinky brown hair, boyishly thin in her jeans, smiled vacuously from her cross-legged perch at one end of the couch. "Everyone, this is our new girl, Justine. Simcha is one of your roommates, Justine."

The frizzy haired, freckled-faced girl waved.

Gina fake whispered, "When Simcha starts going psychotic on you, just get out of her way as quickly as possible."

"Gina!" Lillie yelled, but Simcha wasn't paying attention so Lillie let it go.

I focused on two large bookcases with *Johnny Tremain, The Scarlet Pimpernel, The Bobbsey Twins,* and a set of Landmark biographies.

As we left the TV room, Lillie pointed toward a closed door.

"That's the bedroom for the other cottage parent." Lillie walked on. "There's the telephone room. Girls can make collect calls or receive calls."

She led us to the kitchen and the large "rec room" with windows on three sides, three square tables and straight-back chairs.

"We eat here weekends. All the girls in the cottage have rotating chores to do the washing up and keep the cottage clean." She pointed to a list of chores on the wall:

Pots and pans—Simcha

Sweep—Gina

Wash dishes—Rhonda

Vacuum—Crystal

"During the week we have our meals with the other cottages down in the main dining room." Lillie climbed the stairs and we followed.

"Yoo-hooooo!" she cooed, high-spirited. "We have some young men coming upstairs! Everybody decent?"

The song, *"Young girl, get out of my mind. My love for you is way out of line"* came from the corner room upstairs. A pretty girl—long dirty blonde hair, flecked gray eyes—half reclining on her bed had the song going on a red portable record player.

"Justine, this is Rhonda, your other roommate."

Rhonda put down her *True Confessions* magazine and brightened when the boys came in. She had a big poster of Bob Dylan's head over her bed, the poster where Dylan's wavy hair is in bright psychedelic colors. On her dresser were Breck's crème rinse; shampoo; and a red heart-shaped candy box filled with assorted bobby pins, costume jewelry, a razor, and other junk.

"You like Dylan?" Leo asked.

Rhonda shrugged. "He's okay. Somebody gave me that poster."

Lillie opened a locker built into the wall. "This is your locker, Justine."

"I don't have any clothes with me."

"No problem. We'll get you some tomorrow." I put my mother's hat in the locker.

"We have fourteen girls in this cottage," Lillie said, as she showed us around the other rooms. The upstairs was divided into two sides, with three bedrooms and a communal bathroom on each side.

There were no doors to the girls' bedrooms, just open entryways. Each room had two or three beds, all of them neatly made. At least I wouldn't be sleeping in a barracks.

"And this is my room," Lillie said. "I'm here four nights a week."

Lillie's room was opposite the staircase, next to my room. Through the slightly open door I saw a comfortable yellow armchair, a footstool, a green rug and a framed picture of Jesus Christ.

While Lillie searched for pajamas for me, Rhonda took Leo, Jake, and me downstairs to the porch. Rhonda pointed to the large building adjacent to the cottage.

"That's where we go to school." She half turned and pointed straight ahead. "And there's the infirmary, all the way down there." My brothers nodded politely, but they were watching how nicely she fit into her tight denim shorts and probably didn't notice where the infirmary was.

Rhonda, aware of her audience, and gestured down the hill to a one-story cement building with a smoke stack.

"That's the dining hall." She pointed behind Cottage 6. "And the gym and pool are back there."

The boy who imitated a train was still chugging around the central lawn. "Last stop, 241st Street," he said, coming to a stop.

Rhonda shook her head. "That's Choo-choo Charlie. He knows every train, every line; the IRT, IND, BMT, every local and express stop."

Leo sauntered down the steps. "How long have you been here, Rhonda?"

"Two years."

"What do you think of the place?"

"Too strict. But..." She pointed straight across the square. "That's Cottage 9. My boyfriend Vic lives there. She held up her arm, showing a boy's silver ID bracelet.

"So it's not so bad."

"Yeah."

When it was time for the boys to go, they each gave me a kiss on the cheek.

"Shrimp, if anybody lays a hand on you, tell them you have big brothers and we'll get them," said Jake.

"But you'll be in camp."

"Well, I'll come," said Leo.

"And I'll write to you," said Jake. I nodded. The driver took them to the Thornwood train station. Jake would stay with Leo for a week until he started his summer job as an assistant counselor at Surprise Lake Camp.

That night another cottage parent, quiet, dark-skinned, very buxom Mary, washed my hair at the big kitchen sink.

"You've got big patches of dandruff." Mary used a strong-smelling shampoo and worked her fingers into my scalp. She told me she used to work in a beauty shop, but she didn't say much else. I pictured her as a young girl quietly sweeping up hair in a hair salon for poor Negroes in the south. I hadn't realized my dandruff was so bad, and I didn't know dandruff came in patches. But the smell of the shampoo and Mary's strong massaging fingers comforted me. After she finished with me, my dandruff was gone.

Mary then patiently combed the knots out of Brenda's air. Brenda was so overweight that her blue eyes got lost in her big cheeks. Brenda's black hair was knotted, and Mary sprayed No More Tangles on it, starting from the bottom of her hair, and slowly combed through the knots. Brenda cried while Mary worked on her.

Later Lillie helped me make my bed. "This is how you do hospital corners." Lillie showed me how to put double folds at the corners of the white bottom sheet, to keep it in place. We put another crisp sheet on top, and a fresh pillowcase and blanket. It felt like camp.

When I was in bed but it wasn't lights out yet, Crystal, her orange hair wrapped around giant pink rollers, came into my room and loomed over me, her big breasts showing through her blue baby doll pajamas.

"Listen motherfucka, now get me straight
Your mother's got a pussy like a .248.

It runs by motor.
It runs by gas.
Listen motherfucka, I'm gonna kick your ass."

Crystal ran out, laughing.

"Don't listen to her," Simcha said to me. "She's just playing."

After lights out at nine, things were quiet. Lillie came around with a flashlight, checking in each room to make sure all the girls were in bed.

I lay there, thinking back to when things were better, when it was the four of us living in Queensview. Once when I was four and Jake was ten, Mom had gone to Manhattan for the day and Jake was in charge of me for the day. He made two tuna fish sandwiches on Wonder bread, neatly cut in two, and set the table with two glasses of milk, and two little monkey dishes of plums in syrup with a teaspoon next to it. This perfect lunch seemed like a great achievement to me and I was filled with admiration for him. "You're going to be an economist when you grow up," I told him.

When it had been quiet for a long time, and I knew my roommates were sleeping, I sat up and prayed. "Please God, help me and my mother. Help her get a job. Let her get a nice two-bedroom apartment in Queens that we can afford. Please God, help me. Please God help me."

"Rise and shine, and give God your glory," Lillie crooned the next morning, to wake us. She stood over me. "Justine, you were grinding your teeth last night."

"Grinding my teeth?"

"Like this." She clamped her mouth shut and gnashed her upper teeth against her lower teeth.

"Have you done that before?"

"I don't know…. I dreamed that a woman captured me and was starving me. She wanted me to die."

"Oh, Justine." Lillie sat down on the bed next to me and put her arms around me. "Let's get you a nice breakfast. Nobody's going to hurt you while I'm around."

Lillie checked that we'd made our beds before we all walked down to the dining hall for breakfast. My stomach turned from the dining hall's dirty dishcloth odor.

"It's just for three weeks," I told myself.

We walked through the clatter of 170 noisy kids and dozens of tables to our cottage's three tables. Lillie had me sit next to her and poured me a glass of orange juice from a pitcher. Meanwhile, Brenda went to the kitchen and rolled back a cart filled with silver oblong platters of scrambled eggs and cinnamon toast. Despite the smell and the noise, I liked the food.

Rhonda kept smiling at a boy, about sixteen, dark blond hair, gray eyes, tawny skin, white t-shirt, sleeves rolled up over skinny biceps, a leather wristband, and tight black jeans. That was Vic, and I didn't dare glance at him again.

Lillie frowned at Rhonda over her glasses. "Rhonda, you better keep your eyes to yourself. Stop flaunting yourself before that boy."

Rhonda rolled her eyes and was not sheepish at all from Lillie's reprimand. She smiled to herself, and looked at Vic when she could.

"Justine, after breakfast I'll take you over to the clothing room," Lillie said. "We'll get you some new shoes and fresh clothes."

New clothes and shoes! But I knew it was out of the question. "I don't need shoes. These shoes will be fine until my mother gets me some new ones."

"Well, no one will force you to wear them, but you're getting some new shoes just the same."

While the other girls went to school, Lillie and I went down a slight hill to the clothing room. I decided to keep wearing the clothes I'd arrived in and to change into their clothes only while mine were being washed. They gave me a brown polyester jumper to wear over a blouse, and a pair of yellow denim shorts, a thin lavender cotton bathrobe with a lace-trimmed collar, and pink flowery pajamas, as well as underwear and socks. The loafers on my feet were worn down, and Lillie offered me new brown penny loafers, which I yearned for; but I was compelled to refuse them. It was my duty, like a good trooper, to maintain loyalty to my mother by not accepting anything I didn't absolutely need. Instead I chose ugly black Oxford shoes.

Next Lillie took me to meet my social worker, Miss Schaeffer.

"Now, Miss Schaeffer's only twenty-three, but she's *sharp*. Mm-hmm. Went to Cornell when she was only sixteen."

Miss Schaeffer's office on the second floor of Cottage 11 was bright with huge red and yellow tissue paper flowers on her desk and kids' drawings on the walls. The first thing I noticed was that her complexion had acne scars, but when she smiled her whole face lit up.

"Justine, it's very nice to m-m-m-m-meet you." Miss Schaeffer came around from behind her desk and took my hand. "This has been a t-t-terrible shock for you. How are you d-d-doing?"

"I want to go back to my mother as soon as possible. I don't belong here."

"As soon as your m-m-m-mother gets a job and an apartment you c-c-can go back to her." When she stuttered her whole mouth got caught up, trying to get the words out.

"They had no right to take me away. Just because my mother has some problems, doesn't mean they should take me away from her."

"I understand that you m-m-miss your m-m-m-mother and you're worried about her. But, you were m-m-moving around to a new place night after night. Your mother was k-k-k-k-keeping you out of school."

Miss Schaeffer meant well, but I was exasperated by her inability to understand. We were unusual people. Special. Couldn't she sense that?

"It's not good to go to school every day. People end up like robots. You people are too materialistic. Money isn't everything. Do you realize that my mother always took me to libraries and museums?"

That afternoon was the end of Lillie's five-day shift. "I'm going home to Yonkers and rest myself. You see these gray hairs? You girls gave them to me." A taxi came for her, and Marlboro-chain-smoking, six-foot gaunt-faced Doris Leeds took over. Doris, a generous story teller, told us about how she was so skinny as a kid that she didn't get her period until she was fifteen. I was fond of her immediately, but she didn't have the control over the girls that Lillie did.

That night, after Doris dutifully walked through the rooms with a flashlight, she went downstairs. Shadowy figures emerged from the bedrooms and peeked over the staircase banister, to make sure Doris had gone to bed for the night. The girls and Doris had an unwritten code; if the girls didn't make too much noise, Doris could pretend they weren't up to anything, and she didn't have to bother going upstairs to discipline them.

Jody came to my room first, holding a Kool. "You got a match?" Jody sat on Rhonda's bed, and Rhonda lit her cigarette.

"Lemme get a drag," Rhonda said and Jody passed the cigarette to her. Simcha didn't smoke, but she helpfully opened the windows. She liked the camaraderie.

Crystal came in and sat on my bed, without asking. Gina came in too, smirking.

"Want me to scratch your back, Crystal?"

"Oh, yeah, I need it." Crystal lay down on my bed, on her stomach, and I moved as close to the wall as I could, to get away from them. Gina sat on top of Crystal, put her hands under Crystal's shirt and gently scratched her back in circles. Disgusting girls. I wished they would get off my bed.

Rhonda blew smoke rings out the window. "Simcha, go keep chicky." Someone had to stand by the staircase in case Doris started coming upstairs. If anyone got caught in another girl's bedroom, and especially smoking, she would be restricted to the cottage and not allowed to do activities for a week. Simcha's job was to yell "chicky!" if Doris started coming up the stairs, and everyone would run back to their beds and whoever was smoking would throw the cigarette out the window.

"Okay." Simcha skipped to the stairwell, oblivious to the fact that her frizzy hair was a crazy halo around her head.

"How come you were an emergency case?" Crystal asked.

"Look, I'm just here temporarily. I don't belong here." How long was the back-scratching going to go on?

"Well, everybody's new sometime," said Simcha. "I been here two years."

"I'll be leaving in three weeks."

"Yeah, right." Rhonda flicked her ashes out the window. "She thinks she's too good for this place."

"I have a family," I explained.

Crystal snorted with contempt. "Shut the fuck up, mongloid. You think you're the only person who's got family?"

"Yeah," said Jody, blowing a smoke ring. "If your family is so great, how come you not only came here, but you came as an emergency case?"

"Yeah, *I* didn't come as no emergency case," said Jody.

I was tired, and I wanted them to stop talking. "Can you get off my bed? I'm going to sleep now."

Gina slowly got off Crystal and sat on the windowsill by the foot of my bed, but Crystal stayed on the bed. I pulled the covers higher in as dignified a way as I could.

"Crystal, c'mon, get off Justine's bed," Rhonda said. Crystal did, and Rhonda passed the cigarette to her. "You can have the last drag." Rhonda turned back to me.

"Just tell us why you came here. What's the big secret?"

I chose not to answer.

"You should see Jody's mother," said Crystal.

Jody nodded goofily. "My mother panhandles in Manhattan."

"Where in Manhattan?"

"Midtown, in the Forties and Fifties, on the East Side."

That was my territory. I sat up and looked closely at Jody's face in the dim light from the outside lamppost, taking in her huge eyes, the set of her chin, and saw the resemblance. "Does she have long gray hair. Is she thin? Does she talk to herself and smoke?"

Jody nodded.

"I've seen your mother around for *years*."

"Yeah, right," said Crystal. "There's lots of bag ladies. You don't know it's the same one."

"Her mother is a bag lady without the bags. She walks around Madison Avenue, smoking. Sometimes she screams at people."

Jody nodded. "Yeah."

This poor girl, I thought. Jody's mother was worse than mine. That explained why Jody tore her hair out in her sleep and had to wear a wig.

"We all got fucked-up families," said Rhonda.

I had to say something. It was the fair thing to do. "My mother...we move around a lot. I don't know. My father doesn't send us enough money.... It's difficult, she has emotional problems...." I was careful to emphasize emotional problems. Emotional meant that it was external things that made my mother crazy. If she had mental problems, then it could be in the genes.

"Your father doesn't have the money, right?"

"I don't know.... He remarried and his wife has four sons."

"They're your stepbrothers."

"They're Boy Scouts." The other girls nodded, as though they instantly understood.

"Don't worry. You'll fit in just fine," said Rhonda.

Simcha came in. "Doris just turned her light off," she reported. Now that Doris had gone to bed, they could talk more freely. Simcha started singing in a loud whisper to the tune of Yankee Doodle Dandy. "I'm a juvenile delinquent, I never, never sleep alone...."

Chapter 7

The Nitty Gritty

Three weeks passed and my mother didn't have an apartment or a job, so she got an extension for her hearing. In mid-June Pleasantville's summer activities began. Ken, the dreamboat lifeguard, gave us swimming lessons in the outdoor pool next to the gym. Holding on to the side of the pool, I practiced my kicks and watched older boys make big splashes as they did cannonballs off the diving board. Vic would chase Rhonda around the pool, snapping a towel at her, forcing her to jump in the water.

In Arts & Crafts I made a woven blue-and-white checked potholder out of cloth loops on a metal frame; in wood shop I made a doll's bed; and Ursula, the Swiss knitting teacher, taught me how to knit. She took us to a sewing shop in the town of Pleasantville where a blonde lady in a cardigan helped us pick out any color yarn we wanted.

Ursula patiently taught us to cast on and do the basic knit stitch, and I made a maize-colored scarf for Leo. Ursula helped undo the knitting mistakes of some of the other girls but not for me, because I knitted evenly.

Some of the boys joined the knitting group, just to be near beautiful Ursula.

"Damn, your scarf is ugly," one boy said to another.

"Don't you call my scarf ugly, motherfucka."

"Suffer, dog."

The director of physical education, Mr. Crank, was black and packed with muscles. He was so strong he could afford to be gentle, because even the wildest kids knew he could contain them. We felt safe around him. He started four clubs for girls: jogging, basketball, softball, and a culture club. I joined them all.

Three days a week, after activities, Mr. Crank would take us girls on a mile run around the grounds.

"Breathe in through the nose, out through the mouth. In twice, and exhale twice," he said, demonstrating the pattern. "Get all the air out." We showed him that we got it. "Don't take in too much air," he said. "You don't want to hyper-ventilate. Breathe in slow and steady."

It may not sound like much to run a mile, but it takes a certain amount of concentration. About eight girls would start out on the run, but I was the only one who would finish the course with him.

Mr. Crank would come by the cottage and schmooze with Lillie and flirt with the other cottage parents. But he'd pay attention to the kids too.

He had us playing basketball, doing layups, dribbling, and drills where we ran sideways and passed the ball. We played against other schools for tough or disturbed kids and always got beat. But I loved basketball, because of Mr. Crank.

I was settling into Pleasantville, secretly glad not to be in the hot city. I loved the trees, the fresh air, the birds singing in the morning. The books in the floor-to-ceiling built-in shelves in the TV room were seemingly mine. When I was sitting on the porch bench leaning against the column, *Johnny Tremain* resting on my outstretched legs, I could pretend I was in a privileged boarding school or at camp.

But at PCS you never knew when reality would bring you down to size. Once, I was in my room with Brenda and a big-boned girl from Flatbush. I told them about the time Jake was on *It's Academic*. Out of nowhere, the girl started pounding me on the head. I crumpled on the floor next to the bed, shielding my head with my arms, at the same time thinking, "This is what a beating is like when someone isn't holding back."

"Stop it!" Brenda yelled, pushing the girl off me. I held my head, dazed but glad the punches had stopped.

"If you tell Lillie, I'll kill you," the girl warned. I didn't tell anyone and avoided her after that. She kept to herself pretty much or hung out with Simcha, and lucky for me, she was sent home a few weeks later.

Big-mouthed Dawn came to Cottage 6 a few months after I did. She was only eleven like me, and smart as a whip. I knew that Dawn could "take me." She could kick my ass. Several times Dawn hit me— we competed for Lillie's attention—and I never hit her back. I defended myself with other girls who were bigger and stronger, but I knew Dawn would really hurt me if she got the chance. In early August Dawn set a fire in the bathroom and was sent to a mental hospital. After she was good and gone, Brenda and I happily slapped each other five.

At appointments with Miss Schaeffer I continued to defend my mother.

"My father should pay the rent for an apartment, so we'd always have a place to stay. That way my mother and I won't have to move around all the time."

Miss Schaeffer shook her head.

"I know it's hard, Justine, but I don't think your mother is able to take care of you. Even if the rent would be paid."

That didn't make sense. All we needed was an apartment. Why couldn't Miss Schaeffer see that? She meant well but she was just a social worker.

One night I went to the bathroom and as I came out, Rhonda came in. On the way back to my room I was in a confused stupor, and went into her room, got into *her* bed and fell asleep. When Rhonda came back to her bed she saw me sleeping and laughed because I had walked in my sleep. We lay on the bed talking for hours. Rhonda's window faced the wooden picnic table and trees belonging to Cottage 8, the cottage for the youngest girls, across the way. It had rained, and the trees and grass sparkled.

"What do you want to do when you get out of here?" I asked.

"Have a husband and an apartment," Rhonda said.

"I'm going to college. I want to travel and be a writer."

We were silent for awhile. "Well, that's cool that you want to be a writer. Scratch my back for me?"

She turned on her stomach and I got on top of her and started gently scratching under Rhonda's light pajama top. It had shocked me when I saw other girls scratching each other's backs, but now that I was doing it, it just seemed nice.

I started telling her the story my mother told about the guy who's poor all his life. "When Bontsche dies God says to him, 'You've been a good man. You deserve an award. What do you want?' And Bontsche says, 'All I want is a warm roll with fresh butter every morning.'"

"Fuck that. If that was me, I'd ask for a Rolls Royce. Guy doesn't have anything all his life, now he gets a chance to get something, and he can't even ask for a mansion, and lots of money?"

"But then, why don't you want more than a husband and an apartment?" I said.

Rhonda hesitated. "I don't know. It seems too hard to try for more. But at least it's more than a roll and butter."

One afternoon I was on the porch, leaning against the wall, reading a paperback I found in the rec room, *Dibs In Search of Self,* when Jody and Crystal came outside. Jody carried colored tissue paper and pipe cleaners, her stuff for making paper flowers, and Crystal had two new purplish-gray hickeys on her neck.

Crystal sat down next to me.

"Ugly shoes."

"Ugly hickeys," I said back.

Jody threw a hint of an approving smile in my direction for answering back, as she started rolling the tissue paper into flower petals.

"My *boyfriend* gave them to me. When a boy gives you a hickey it means he really *likes* you, and I really like him. Get it?"

"But Lillie says, 'Don't let any boy mark you.'"

"Shut the fuck up, dipshit. *Bookworm.*" Crystal slapped *Dibs* out of my hands. "I bet you've never even made out with a boy."

"No. But you better be careful when you do that. You don't want to get pregnant."

Jody stopped twirling the tissue paper into petals. "What are you talking about?"

"Well, why do you think poor people have so many children when they can't afford them? Because they can't resist putting their arms around each other and kissing. And something from a man's body crosses over to the woman's body, and you know, gets into her vagina. And then she gets pregnant. And that's why people sometimes have eight or nine children, and then they're stuck and can't take care of them." I liked teaching kids and sharing my wisdom gained from all those hours reading in the Donnell Library. "I mean, aren't you afraid of getting pregnant?"

There were a few moments of silence while Jody and Crystal came to understand my stunning ignorance of sex and reproduction. In those long seconds they looked at each other, checking to be sure that such stupidity was really possible; meanwhile, it hit me like a lightning bolt—the penis went into the vagina. The girls were right. There was so much I didn't know.

Crystal bent over, laughing. "H-h-how are babies made?"

Jody could barely get the words out. "By making out!" Jody's eyes weren't looking so mournful just then.

Crystal sashayed around, laughing, twirling, and she looked across the square toward Cottage 9, hoping to see some boys. She gleefully started chanting as she paraded around the porch:

I come from PCS, oh pity me.
There's not a decent boy in the vicinity!
And every night at nine they lock the doors.
I don't know why the hell I ever came before.

I'm gonna pack my bags and roam about.
I'm gonna turn this whole place upside down.
I'm gonna smoke and drink and neck and peck and what the heck,
The hell with the PCS!

The girls kept looking across the square, and I looked too, to see if Crystal would get some attention. As I watched, I realized a taxi was slowly moving around the square, coming in our direction, and the familiar sense of dread came over me, when you see trouble coming and you can't do anything to stop it. My mother's large-brimmed hat came into view, and she waved her hand out the window to me. It wasn't Sunday, visiting day; it was just a weekday, and she wasn't allowed to be here.

I knew and accepted without thinking about it, that the taxi must have cost fifty dollars or more to come all the way here from Manhattan. Money that could have been saved up for an apartment deposit and month's rent. She must have gotten a check from her brother, Uncle Sam, and couldn't resist the impulse to just get here.

Mom got out of the taxi carrying a Gimbel's shopping bag. Her white blouse had a small coffee stain on the front, and a button on her jacket was loose. But as I walked up to her I saw that she had on lipstick.

"Who's that?" Crystal asked.

I didn't answer, just kissed my mother on the cheek. She was grayer at the temples.

"Mom, you know you're not allowed to do this. You'll get in trouble."

"I miss you. Help me with my bags. Here, I brought you some cookies and fruit."

Mom always had food for me, but the package would almost always be opened. It was rare for Mom to give me something that she hadn't allowed herself to taste. She paid the driver and he drove away.

"I was worried about you. I walk around, I see other children that remind me of you, and I keep thinking, 'Why was my little Justine taken from me?' I can't understand how this happened. Here, have some raisins."

"I had a snack."

"Well, have another one. Let's go sit on the bench."

As we walked toward the picnic bench on the lawn next to the house, Lillie opened the door to the porch and walked down the steps. I hoped Mom wouldn't insult Lillie.

"Mrs. Blau, hello."

Mom nodded slightly in my direction, mumbling under her breath, *"Meshuganah."* Mom ignored Lillie and motioned for me to follow her. "Let's go."

As we began walking away, a car pulled up and the supervisor Mr. Sladen got out. He was large, had a thick black moustache, and his bald head looked so hard it reminded me of a bowling ball. He was known for giving kids "noogies"—he'd get a kid in a choke hold, move his big gold ring to his knuckle, and knock them on the head with it.

Mom took a look at him. "Assess the situation and act accordingly," she said to me.

"Mrs. Blau, you know you're not allowed to come up like this," Mr. Sladen said, moving closer. "Visiting Day is Sunday." Couldn't he understand that she needed help? He was making a mistake coming on like an authority figure.

"This is my daughter. Not your daughter," Mom said, putting her arm around me. "Who are you to tell me when I can see her?"

"You can come up on Sunday like the other parents."

My mother held up her hand imperiously. "I need a few minutes with my daughter."

"You can talk to her for a minute, Mrs. Blau. Then I'm taking you to the train station."

She turned her back to him. "A *bulvan*," she said under her breath, using the Yiddish term for a person without spiritual graces. "Okay, Justine. Here are the raisins and cookies."

Mom took a few cookies out of the bag before handing me the rest. "I need something to eat on the train." She put the cookies into a napkin and tucked them into her purse.

"How are they treating you?" Mom looked at me intently, focusing on me.

"Fine, Mom. Okay."

"You're still my little girl?"

"Of course, Mom."

She handed me an envelope with quarters. "Here's some change so you can call me."

"Mom, I don't know where you're staying."

"As soon as I get a permanent place I'll send you the phone number."

"Okay."

"I love you."

"I love you too."

Mr. Sladen opened the door of his car and walked toward us. "Mrs. Blau?"

"We'll be back together soon, Justine."

"Okay."

Mom got in the back seat. As they drove away my mother rolled down her window and blew a kiss at me.

Rhonda and Crystal watched us closely.

"Your mother's a bag lady." Crystal's disgusting cleavage showed.

"Shut up."

Lillie intervened. "Crystal, you know better than that. Go upstairs!"

"It's not my fault her mother's a bag lady."

A surge overtook me. "My mother is *educated*," I snarled. "Your mother is *nothing* compared to my mother."

Crystal slapped me, and I grabbed at her face, scratching her cheek. We flailed at each other until Lillie tore us apart.

"That's enough!" Lillie shouted.

Crystal's cheek was bleeding, and she was shaking. It was sheer luck that I made her bleed.

"Your ass is grass!" Crystal yelled.

"Nobody's ass is anything, do you hear me?" Lillie said, pushing Crystal toward the door. "And I'll slap you upside your head myself if you hit anybody again. You don't call someone's mother a bag lady."

"Yeah, well, she looks like one." Crystal touched her cheek and saw the blood.

"Go upstairs and wash your face," Lillie said.

Crystal finally went in.

Lillie took my hand and slowly led me up the stairs. "Get your brush, and I'll brush your hair," she said. I got it and went to her room. On Lillie's dresser was a photo of her late husband, a teacher, who'd become blind in later life. Lillie sat in her worn yellow armchair, and I sat in front of her and Lillie brushed my long brown hair.

"How are you doing, sweetheart?"

"I'm okay, Lillie."

"Your hair is your crowning glory," Lillie said, stroking my hair as she brushed. As the brush slid through my hair I leaned against her knees, relaxing somewhat.

After awhile she put the brush down and kissed my forehead.

Chapter 8

Psychology and Cookies

The time was coming up for the court to decide whether I would be kept at Pleasantville or sent back to my mother. The judge needed a psychological evaluation of me to make a decision, so I was sent to a psychologist in Scarsdale for tests.

The quiet man drove me in the Black Maria. This was my first time in the car since I was taken from my mother, when Leo and Jake had gone with me in the car up to Pleasantville, to make sure I'd be okay there. But my brothers were coming to visit me less often.

The driver stopped at a large fieldstone house nestled among trees and hedges. It was just the kind of place I had fantasized living in for years, with details I remembered from the apartment ads in the Sunday real estate section of *The New York Times:* stained glass and bay windows. A Lorna Doone house.

Dr. Bloomingdale, the psychologist, had her office on the side with a separate entrance.

On the wall were framed degrees—one from Radcliffe—and a portrait of Freud. She sat at her desk across from me. She was tan, self-assured, and wore a silver and turquoise Indian necklace, the kind I used to pine over at Teepee Town across from the Forty-Second Street library.

"Tell me about yourself, Justine."

How should I answer? I could say, "I was taken away from my mother after living in hotels for six years, and as you know I'm living in an institution with juvenile delinquents and emotionally disturbed children." But she knew all that.

"I like to read Louisa May Alcott books, and I want to work in the Peace Corps when I grow up."

"Why are you living at the Pleasantville Cottage School?"

I wondered if, being a psychologist, she could see through me and know what I was thinking. That I desperately wanted someone to save me.

"My mother and I didn't have an apartment to live in, and we're waiting until we get one."

"Hmm. So that's why you're living at Pleasantville, because you're waiting for an apartment?"

It was hard to explain. "It's complicated. My mother has problems. We move around a lot. Hopefully one day we'll have a nice apartment. My father should help us more."

"How is it at Pleasantville?"

"It's all right. At least there are children there."

"You like being with other children."

I nodded.

"Tell me about your father."

"He's a stockbroker. But I'd rather not talk about him."

"Why?"

"It's unpleasant to do so." I hoped she got from my haughtiness that I was more refined than the other Pleasantville kids. I didn't have a father who loved me but I deserved a father who loved me.

"What do you wish for?"

"I would like to leave PCS. I'd like to have a nice home in California. And to have a happy life when I'm older."

Dr. Bloomingdale asked me to draw my family.

"Should I draw all of it?" I didn't know if I was supposed to include my father.

"Yes."

"Should I include myself?"

"Yes."

I drew myself in the far right-hand corner. Next to me I drew Jake, his straight brown hair a little long because we couldn't afford haircuts, his thick glasses, slightly bulbous nose. The checked button-down shirt, top button open. Then my mother, plump, in a floral dress with her big purse; then Leo, the tallest, his curly black hair, his glasses, and his shirt similar to Jake's. The four of us were together with arms interlocked, Jake between me and my mother. I drew my father separate from the group of us, not touching.

Dr. Bloomingdale looked at the drawing. "Hmm."

"What is it?" I asked.

She hesitated, then pointed to the drawing of my father. "You gave your father and yourself matching shirts, belts, cuffs, and eyebrows."

"What does that mean? Is that wrong?"

"No, it's not wrong. It means you feel a connection with him."

I had the sense that psychology was really interesting.

Next Dr. Bloomingdale brought out a card with a picture of a girl. "Justine, can you make up a story about this person?"

I looked at the girl and immediately knew her story.

"She feels left out, but a nice man is going to come and give her presents, which will make her feel better."

She showed me another picture, of a woman and a girl.

I launched right in. "They're a mother and daughter, but they're disagreeing about something. The girl fakes the mother out and does what *she* wants. This girl just wants to be a kid. The girl has a toy that she wants to keep, but her mother wants her to give it away."

The last picture was of a girl and a box. "The girl is very unhappy because she thinks no one loves her. One day this package arrived. It's a very expensive present from a boy she had once rejected. She is very sorry she had been so snobbish to him. She accepts the present, and they're friends again."

After the tests were over, I had to wait until the driver came to pick me up in the Black Maria. I sat outside on the stone wall and took out the scarf I was knitting. After a few minutes Dr. Bloomingdale came to the window overlooking the wall.

"Would you like some milk and cookies?" The tests had taken hours, and I was hungry but I shook my head no. I had the sense that the psychologist felt sorry for me. Instead I wanted her to show that she was touched by my pluck, that she cared about me by making a warmer offer. I wanted Dr. Bloomingdale to make it possible for me to accept the cookies, to insist, "Come, honey, have some cookies," in case I changed my mind. But she didn't, and I couldn't bring myself to retract and tell her that in fact I really wanted those cookies.

"No thanks." I maintained my dignity, knitting on the stone wall, waiting for the Black Maria to pick me up.

Chapter 9

Sneaking Out

Rhonda was always running: away from cottage parents, or across the square to see Vic. Once in the middle of the night I woke up when Rhonda ran into our room, breathless, back from sneaking out. In the dim light from the porch I saw her peel off her wet tank top and denim cutoffs, down to her nylon bikini panties and bra. For a moment Rhonda gazed through the open window in the direction of Vic's cottage and raised her wrist to kiss his silver ID bracelet.

Before Rhonda had snuck out a few hours ago, she'd stuffed clothes under the covers, to make it look like she was in bed. Now she took her blue-and-yellow daisy baby doll pajamas from the heap and put them on.

"Did you go in the pool?" I whispered.

Rhonda ignored me and wrapped her wet hair with a towel, like a turban. She was self-destructive but not enough to risk confiding in me.

"I won't tell anyone. I promise."

Rhonda came over to my bed and leaned over me. "Shut the fuck up, Justine," she said softly. Swiftly Rhonda threw her wet sneakers and clothes under her bed and got in. She glanced at Simcha who was breathing evenly; but even if Simcha was faking sleep, she would never snitch.

A few minutes later, Lillie's phone rang. I heard the murmur of her voice. She had probably been reading *Ebony*, resting her fifty-five-year-old self in her chair, her feet up on a stool. Watching over her on the wall was her beloved Jesus.

Lillie hung up the phone and locked the door to her room, angrily jangling her keys. She marched to our room, flicking on the ceiling light. She took off the granny glasses that she wore on a chain around her neck and leveled her Georgia glare at Rhonda.

"Get up, Rhonda! Get up and get dressed!"

"Lillie, what happened?" Rhonda tried to look sleepy.

Lillie sucked her teeth. "If you keep this up, Rhonda, they're going to send your sorry behind to Hawthorne. You mark my words, girl." The Hawthorne Cedar Knolls School was where really tough kids got sent. Linda, a girl from our cottage with a low voice and big hips had been sent to the Hawthorne Cedar Knolls School, and we'd heard she'd been stabbed with an ice pick.

Now get up!"

"Lillie—"

"Don't add your lies on top of this mess, Rhonda. We know what you were up to." Lillie swooped down on Rhonda and pulled the wet turban off her hair.

"Ow," Rhonda whined. "I washed my hair tonight."

Simcha woke up and watched.

"You wet your hair over at the main building, gallivanting around with boys, spraying fire extinguishers. There's four inches of water on the main floor. Now put your clothes on! Lord, it grieves me how you can't get control of yourself, Rhonda. Mr. Sladen's coming for you, and you're going to clean up over there."

I watched but kept the sheet over most of my face to hide my satisfaction over Rhonda getting caught.

Rhonda got out of bed slowly. Lillie opened Rhonda's locker and shoved the clothes to the side.

"Where are the wet clothes?" Lillie squinted her eyes and thrust her face into Rhonda's. "Where's your shame? You dragged Mr. Sladen and me and all these other people out of their beds."

Rhonda slumped and got down on her knees next to her bed and pulled her sopping clothes from underneath. Lillie took the clothes and watched as Rhonda, deflated, started dressing.

"Can I have some privacy while I put my bra on?"

"Just turn towards the wall and put that bra on. You think you're a woman, girl?"

Rhonda and the others—Vic, Rozzie Eisenstein, Bruce Quinn, and Seth Rosen—had to mop up the water for hours and were grounded for a month.

For Rhonda, being grounded was tough. She missed seeing Vic during activities time at night, seven to nine. Instead she had to stay home with younger kids like me, having chocolate pudding and watching *I Dream of Jeannie* and *Flipper* in our pajamas.

Every Saturday night the boys in Cottage 9 hosted a teen lounge in their basement. Robert Chernow, the self-appointed dee-jay, was the first person I ever saw wearing bellbottoms, tight striped ones, and Nehru collars. He was as good-looking as Neal Cassidy, thin with high cheekbones, his long hair a shimmer of golden brown. Once he took Rozzie Eisenstein out to see *Bonnie and Clyde* in town, her first real date. She said he was a gentleman.

Robert had set up Cottage 9's basement with a giant wooden box about four feet high. On top was a record player, and inside the box were cushions on the bottom where boys and girls made out. Robert set up a black light, turning the white in everyone's clothes, teeth and eyes luminescent. I watched the other kids slow dance to "Cherish," "When a Man Loves a Woman," and the other 45s Robert played.

Rhonda was restless, missing out on this action. She wanted to sneak out again to see Vic, but the other girls wouldn't go with her. Rhonda's wildness had an edge that made even PCS kids hesitate.

Being surrounded by older girls, who had breasts and wore bras, I was ashamed that I didn't have either. I went to the clothing room but they didn't have any training bras, just a white size AA cup that was too big. I took it back to my room, and, sitting on my bed, carefully cut the tips off the cups to make them less pointed. Brenda came by my room as I was sewing the second cup closed with pink thread. I tried to taper the ends, so the cup would be smooth. I was proud of my self-reliance until I saw Brenda's look of contempt, and I realized the bra was tacky. I had a sense of vagueness—I didn't quite understand about training bras and I thought there was something wrong with my breasts. I was angry that finding a training bra was such a hurdle.

In August Dad sent me a box of Droste pastille chocolates, a souvenir from his summer vacation in Canada with Gisela and her sons. I gave the chocolates out to the girls and didn't have any myself.

There was a letter in the package asking if he could visit me on a Sunday. I wrote him back:

Father,

Henceforth, do not write to me again. I disown you.
Justine

One night soon after, Rhonda hounded me to sneak out with her. "I need someone to keep chicky."

"Not me."

"You know, if you want me to look out for you, you gotta back me up too. Come on. It'll be fun."

"No. I don't want to." But I liked being in good with Rhonda. Finally I agreed to go along.

That night I wore regular clothes to bed instead of pajamas. Around midnight both Rhonda and Crystal shook me.

"Justine, come on, wake up!" Rhonda whispered. I opened my eyes and closed them again, regretting that I had gotten myself into this.

"Justine!"

"You've got Crystal, you don't need me."

Rhonda prodded me. "You're keeping chicky."

I knew it was more fun for them to sneak out in a group rather than to be out in the dark by themselves.

"Let's go," said Crystal. She was crazy about Vic's friend Neal DeAngelis, who also lived in Cottage 9.

I got out of bed. Crystal looked at me in my skirt. "Douche bag. You for real?"

Rhonda opened my dresser drawer. "This isn't 'Gidget Sneaks Out,'" she whispered. "You can't wear a skirt."

"My mother told me not to take any clothes from this place. "

"Later for that." Crystal reached over Rhonda, grabbed new jeans from the clothing room that I had never worn, and tossed them at my head.

"Put them on. The boys are waiting."

Rhonda tossed me a black top. "And you wear dark colors when you sneak out."

We tiptoed through the hall to the end bedroom. The three girls sleeping there didn't hear us as we entered their room and opened the fire escape door. Crystal put a wad of paper towels under the door so it wouldn't completely shut, and we ran down the metal steps.

We dodged a bright light on the side of the cottage, dashing to an unlit area. Instead of going directly across the square, we avoided porch lights by running around the outer cottages, across the road lined with high trees. We stayed on the PCS grounds, but if we wanted to leave, there were no gates to stop us. It was hot, but a breeze blew among the trees, and I felt a wave of relief that I was on this leafy campus rather than being stuck in the sweltering city.

A car came on the central road, its headlights on. We lay on the ground until it passed.

When we reached Cottage 9, Crystal threw gravel at Neal's window. He waved, and in a few minutes he appeared with Vic and Bruce Quinn behind. Vic was a masculine version of Rhonda. He wore tight black jeans and his t-shirt sleeves rolled up. Skinny but brash.

"Hey you, twerp," he whispered. "How are babies made?"

"By making out!" Neal snorted convulsively. They all laughed, quietly.

We ran through some woods to a field and sat under a tree. Neal had curly black hair and was short with extremely thick, muscular thighs and arms and a barrel chest. He was about fifteen, but to me he was a man. He and Crystal started making out, and Vic and

Rhonda lay down together. What if this boy Bruce tried anything with me? And if he didn't, what would we say to each other?

Neal reached under Crystal's blouse and felt her breasts. She pushed his hand away, but he put it back. They did this until she let him keep it there. After awhile they lay down on the grass. I moved away.

Bruce sat near me on the grass. I'd seen him around. He was twelve years old, and the cowlick in his straight brown hair reminded me of Alfalfa from *The Little Rascals*, but he wasn't as goofy.

"I'm not doing anything," I said, ripping at the grass.

"Who asked you?"

I didn't know what to say.

He pretended to throw a ball. "Do you like the Mets?"

I shrugged. I knew of the Mets vaguely.

"That's my team. Best team in the world. You know Tom Seaver, the pitcher?"

"Yeah. I've heard of him."

"Tom Terrific. That's his nickname. They were in last place, and now they've won eight games and have a shot at the pennant. Because of him." I liked his voice.

"My grandmother takes me to games sometimes."

"Oh." That was sweet. I wondered why he didn't live with his grandmother, instead of here.

He was okay. He wasn't going to make a move on me, and he was being nice. I breathed a little easier. I pulled a large blade of grass and put it between my thumbs, cupped my hands like Jake had taught me, and blew on it, making a shrill sound. I thought it might impress Bruce.

"Hey, that's good for a girl," Bruce said.

"Be quiet!" whispered Vic. "We'll get caught!"

Bruce moved closer to me. "Show me how you do that," he said softly. He probably wasn't as smart as my brothers, but he was enough like them. He tore a blade of grass, and I showed him how to place it between his thumbs.

"What do you do with your lips?" he whispered. I pursed my lips and he quickly leaned close and kissed me. I laughed out loud. He smiled so endearingly.

"You tricked me," I said, but I was pleased.

Suddenly a guard yelled and light from a flashlight spun wildly around us.

"Chicky!" the other kids yelled, and we ran toward the dining hall.

"What are you doing there? Stop!" The guard ran toward us.

"My dogs come to me!" Neal taunted him. We dashed across the basketball court, past the colonnade, and then we split up, the boys in one direction, the girls in the other. The boys chanted as they sped off:

Oo, oongawa, Jew power
I said it, I meant it,
I'll even represent it.
I'm a cool, cool Jew
From a cool, cool town
Takes another cool Jew
To knock me down.
You don't like my star
Don't shake my tree.
I'm a New York Jew

Don't mess with me!

The guard followed us, the girls, because we ran slower. We ran past the dining room, along the administration building, but soon he was catching up to us. Rhonda was far ahead.

All those nights when I traipsed around with my mother, schlepping shopping bags, and I would desperately wish for a bed to sleep in. So why had I left my safe bed tonight, when no one forced me to?

The rattling of the guard's keys came closer. As we approached the gym and the outdoor pool, he grabbed my arm.

"Got ya!" he exulted. He was black, young, in his twenties, and wore his hair in an Afro.

"Rhonda, help!" I yelled. Rhonda stopped, while Crystal escaped.

The road was lit by the light from the outside of the administration building. We caught our breath in the heat as Rhonda slowly walked back and came up beside me.

"Oo, look at you." The guard leered at her.

Rhonda rolled her eyes.

"What were you girls up to?"

"We were taking a walk," said Rhonda. "Can't you just let us go? We'll go right back to our cottage."

"A walk? Mm-hmm. With those boys?"

"No," Rhonda said quietly.

"You like being with boys, huh?" The guard took out his handcuffs.

"You know what I could do right now? I could knock you out and take both of you right here."

Rhonda and I became very still. It didn't even occur to me to run. I knew he could overpower me.

"Let's not get carried away," said Rhonda.

"Yup, that's what I could do, take you both."

"Assess the situation and act accordingly," I recited, trying to look stern. "I'm only eleven years old," I said. "If you do that, you'll ruin my life."

"You're only eleven." Suddenly he didn't look so smug. "Shit. Jailbait."

I pulled Rhonda's arm out of his grip. "Yeah, you *f'shtinkener.*" I used the low, authoritative voice my brothers had coached me to use when I played Merlin. "Don't touch me! Or her."

"Okay." He laughed, shaking his head. "Eleven. Shit." He put his handcuffs back. "I'll walk you to your cottage."

We walked silently. When we reached the cottage we ran up the fire escape stairs.

After we were in our beds awhile, still wound up, Rhonda whispered, *"F'shtinkener.* That's a good one."

"You came back for me. Thanks," I said.

"You think I'm a *f'shtinkener?* I wouldn't have left you flat."

Being at the mercy of the security guard, feeling we couldn't tell someone that he had threatened us with rape, was subduing. It added to my feeling of helplessness, and I never snuck out again. But compared to all the nights when my family had no place to sleep and trudged the streets, so tired, and all the years of being broke and ashamed, this was just a blip, a momentary scare.

As the summer continued, my mother still hadn't gotten a job or an apartment. She got extension after extension for her hearing to get me back.

School started in September, and my sixth-grade teacher was Mr. Palmieri, a former Yonkers policeman.

In my class of ten kids, the only other girl was thin, quiet, adorable Vivian Klingsberg, from Cottage 8. Her huge brown eyes were so plaintive and expressive, I always felt like rescuing her. She brushed her straight brown hair obsessively and was a perfectionist in class. She studied intensely for spelling tests and had to get 100s. We became close friends. I would often walk Vivian over to the infirmary where the nurses would give her the huge, black lithium pill she was supposed to take every night. The nurses always checked her mouth to make sure she swallowed it.

"They make me feel like a zombie," Vivian complained. The nurses were understanding, but when Vivian didn't take the pill, she could get agitated. I worried that if we had a fight, it would embarrassing if she could take me, since I was a year older.

The nurses liked Vivian and me, and they took us out a few times for Chinese food in Yonkers.

Bruce Quinn was also in Mr. Palmieri's class. When we weren't in class, I hoped to catch sight of him. That was one of the reasons I volunteered to keep Vivian company when she went to the infirmary for her pill, because our route passed by his cottage. I joined the synagogue choir because Bruce was in it. We sang "Hail to the Cockroach" instead of "Hail to the Conqueror," annoying the kindly choirmaster.

I began running laps around the square on my own, to build up my stamina and win Mr. Crank's approval. Also because I would pass Cottage 9 with every lap, hoping that Bruce saw me and admired me for running.

Miss Schaeffer started a girls group with some of us—Brenda, Crystal, Jody, Simcha, Gina and me—to talk about life at PCS.

In the first session we started talking about Brenda getting into a fight with Jody. The fight started when Brenda wrapped gum around her own hair. Mary spent hours cutting the gum out, and she had to cut Brenda's hair very short. When Jody teased Brenda about it, Brenda punched her.

Jody brought it up. "What the hell did you punch me for?"

Brenda shook her head, stricken.

"Brenda, c-c-can I tell the girls what happened with your foster f-f-f-amily this week?" Miss Schaeffer asked her. Brenda shrugged. Miss Schaeffer paused to give Brenda time to think about it.

"Okay, with your permission I'll tell them." Miss Schaeffer looked at us. "Brenda's foster parents told her she couldn't go home for Rosh Hashanah weekend. Brenda feels that they let her down, abandoned her. Do you think that might have anything to do with this incident?"

"Oh, get over yourself," I blurted out. "Stop feeling sorry for yourself. You make me sick." Everyone looked at me surprised.

"Fuckin' bitch." Brenda lunged toward me, but Miss Schaeffer grabbed her and got between us.

"Sit down, Brenda. We'll talk this through," Miss Schaeffer said.

Brenda slowly sat down.

"Okay, what's going on here?"

Brenda just shook her head.

Miss Schaeffer looked at me. "What's going on with you?"

"*Me?* I don't have a problem. It's just that she's such a crybaby."

"You said she's feeling sorry for herself," said Miss Schaeffer. "Are you feeling sorry for *your*self?"

"Why are we talking about *her?*" said Brenda. "We started out talking about me."

"We'll get back to talking about you," Miss Schaeffer assured Brenda. "I promise."

"Why are you feeling sorry for yourself, Justine?"

"My mother is crazy. I hate her."

Brenda had a vicious look. "You have no right to feel sorry for yourself!" she yelled. "You have two brothers. And your mother isn't as bad as mine. At least she *wants* you. And your father sends you things and you're too stupid to take them. I don't even know my father. My mother met my father at Roseland. I was conceived in the parking lot behind Roseland."

She sat quietly, tears streaming down her face.

"I think you are all realizing how terribly that would hurt, to have no one," Miss Schaeffer said.

There was quiet for a few moments.

"But you're not alone, Brenda," Simcha said. "You gotta believe you're gonna have somebody else to love. You gotta learn to make friends. And you have us. We'll help you and sometimes you'll help us."

At another session of the girls group Simcha was rocking back and forth, then jumping up to look out the window, acting crazy.

Some of the girls were kind of laughing and Simcha got wilder, running around the room. Miss Schaeffer yelled.

"I thought you were here to help each other. You're just encouraging her to act out!"

The girls were silent.

"You mean, you expect us to try to stop her when she acts crazy?" Jody twirled strands of her wig hair nervously.

Miss Schaeffer turned to Simcha, "What do you expect from them?"

"Well, they should help me if they're my friends."

"But when we try to stop you from acting crazy you get mad at us and you turn on us," said Brenda.

Simcha admitted it. "Yeah, I can't take it very much, but don't give up."

I didn't see how Brenda could survive. It was too hard to go on without family. I was lucky to have my brothers. And even my mother, compared to hers. And my father. He was there in the background.

In November I got a fever and was sent to the infirmary. Coincidentally, Bruce was there too. For three days we drank apple juice and chewed orange-flavored Aspergum, flirting in a slightly feverish, delirious, easy cocoon. He took the wooden stick out of the leather ponytail holder in my hair and tickled me with it.

I wrote him a letter talking about the "hot stick" and the nurses found it and showed it to Lillie, concerned about what the hot stick was. I indignantly explained that it was just an innocent pony tail holder.

Chapter 10

Running Away

One Sunday morning I went to the bottom of the hill with Vivian and her younger, scrawny brother, Tom, to wait for their grandmother who always came on the eleven o'clock bus. My mother had telephoned that she would be on the bus too.

The first person off the bus was a girl about eight years old who grabbed our attention with her long messy blonde hair, fringed white leather jacket, and matching go-go boots. "Pussy galore, pussy galore," she said softly as she passed by us, following her mother. They were Gina's mother and sister. Pussy Galore was a character in the movie *Goldfinger*, but I didn't know that and maybe the girl didn't either.

Next was a heavyset lady wearing a net over curlers in her hair, followed by Vivian's tiny grandmother, nondescript except for her green knit hat, clutching a mesh bag. Vivian and Tom clung to her as they made their way up the hill.

My mother appeared, more disheveled than ever. I kissed her cheek and took her Alexander's shopping bag to make it easier for her to walk up the hill. We walked apart from the others.

"Are you all right, Mom?"

"How can I be all right when my daughter's been taken from me? Like I was one of those mothers who abuses her kids?" She sneered toward the other relatives, saying that the fat lady and the girl in go-go boots were planted there to harass her, to force her to acknowledge that she belonged to an inferior class of people who can't take care of their children.

"It's not so bad here, Mom."

"That's not the point. You belong to me."

We walked awhile in silence.

"You look pretty," I said.

"You say that, but you don't really care for me anymore."

We reached the big lawn.

"Do you want to see my room?"

"No, I don't want to go in that place. Let's sit down somewhere outside." I steered her toward the colonnade and we sat on a bench in the shade.

"Have you been looking for an apartment?"

"How can I find an apartment? I have no money. That monster..." She sighed and looked distant. Then she turned back to me. "So, what do you do here?"

"Well, I'm in school."

"Oh, right."

"And I'm making friends. That's Vivian over there."

"You're selling out, aren't you? You're becoming one of 'them.'"

"No, I'm not."

"You're turning away from me," she practically yelled. "You're cold. I don't know you anymore. You're even wearing the clothes they gave you. I told you not to." I was wearing the yellow shorts and a top they'd given me.

"Mom, I had nothing else to wear."

"Oh bullshit!"

My mother almost never used bad language, and her cursing now stunned me.

"You betrayed me, Justine. You took their clothes. You're on their side."

"Mom, no. I'm on your side. But they said if you just find an apartment and get a job you can have me back."

"You're an ungrateful child! Don't you understand that I'd get better if you came back to me?"

I felt so bad for her. I wished there were a hundred of me so I could give her one.

"A mother and daughter should be together whether I have a job or not. You're going away with me today. You can help me find a job."

"I can't," I said. "We have to wait until the hearing."

"I need you, Justine. We have to stick together."

"Mom, please, can't you find a job on your own?"

"Let's go, Justine."

"I don't want to. I'm sick of living in hotels. I want to stay here until you get an apartment."

"Enough!" Her fury was formidable to me. "People have to sacrifice for their families sometimes. I've certainly sacrificed enough for you."

She took my hand.

"Please Mommy. I don't want to go."

She pulled her hand away. "Don't call me 'mommy.' You don't act like my daughter. You act like I'm your aunt."

"Mom, I'm afraid you'll get arrested."

Her face softened. "Oh! You're worried about me." She took my hand again. "Don't worry, Justine. I'll risk it for you."

"But Mom, what if they put you in handcuffs again?"

"Let's get out of here."

She pulled me slightly, and that's all it took. I went with her, back the way we had come.

On the way off grounds we passed Choo-Choo Charlie steering his train around the square. "Thirty-Fourth Street, Pennsylvania Station. Next stop, Fourteenth Street Seventh Avenue." He drove with all his concentration.

My mother and I walked down the hill, and when we reached the bottom, she started hitchhiking. A few cars passed and kept going. After awhile, one stopped and Mom got in. I held back.

"Come on, Justine."

"Mommy, we'll get in trouble."

"You're my little girl. It's okay."

I backed off. "No, Mom."

She turned harsh. "Justine! Now!" I got in and the car took off.

The driver took us as far as Yonkers and dropped us outside a grocery store. It was dusk; the world seemed vast, lonely, empty. We somehow found a taxi that took us to the northernmost subway station in the Bronx, 241st Street. That night we ended up at a second-rate hotel in Manhattan.

Mom and I went through our routine of taking the twin-sized mattress off the box spring and putting the top sheet on the box spring. We were both tired. I wondered what the other girls were doing. Having their showers, getting snack (Sunday night it was fried pepperoni on toast), and watching *Bonanza*. I missed my lavender bathrobe that they'd given me, and I wanted my toothbrush and my own bed. I missed knowing where I would have breakfast and what the plan for tomorrow would be. I desperately wanted to go back.

"Mom, I'm going to the bathroom. Do you have any toothpaste? I'll use my finger to brush my teeth."

"It's in my bag. I'll buy you a toothbrush tomorrow."

I found the toothpaste and went out into the hallway to use the communal bathroom. It was so dismal.

Back in the room I turned off the light without asking her if it was okay. I lay down on the mattress on the floor. A police siren wailed in the distance.

"Mom, maybe that's the police after us."

"No, don't worry, they're not after us."

I stared up at the shifting pattern of shadows that the outside lights made on the wall. The siren got louder and the shadows shook intensely until the squad car passed by and they began to subside.

My mother started humming the tune her father sang to her. *"Rings on your fingers, bells on your toes..."*

"Justine, things will get better."

I didn't say anything.

We were on the run for a month. My father stopped sending her alimony checks, since she had "kidnapped" me. Our money was lower than ever.

We stayed a night at the Pennsylvania Hotel. The next day we didn't return the key, hoping the room wouldn't be rented and we could sleep there again. We returned to the room at nine that night and it was empty. No one had checked in. We put the chain on the door, in case someone did show up, and went to sleep. Around ten someone put a key in the lock and tried to get in. The chain kept them from opening it completely, and they were puzzled. They went downstairs, which gave us a few minutes to hastily pack up our stuff and get out.

"You're my good little trooper," my mother told me.

"I'm your good little schlepper," I thought to myself. That night I dreamt that my mother was chasing me.

Mom called information and got the phone number of a boy-friend from her teenage years, Ben Hoffman. He was married with two daughters. We spent that night with them at their Brooklyn home.

"We're in between apartments," Mom told them.

They were nice people. They knew nothing of Pleasantville.

I slept on a cot in a bedroom with the girls. I understood that they were entitled to this home, and I was not. The family had two copies of a beautiful hard-covered book, *Anthology of Children's Literature*, and they gave me one. This was a splendid gift, and it kept me company during that miserable month of wandering.

The Waldorf Hotel ladies' room was elegant with a peach-and-cream patterned wallpaper, a flower arrangement on a counter, and a tray with perfume, deodorant and powder.

Mom and I washed up. But whereas I did it quickly and effi-ciently, she closed her eyes, leaned her head back a little and washed her neck slowly, relishing the simple pleasure. The attendant dabbed at a few wet spots on the counter disapprovingly, knowing she wouldn't be getting a tip. To my mother the attendant was not even a speck in the universe.

"Wash under your arms, Justine."

"Mom, no!"

The attendant reluctantly handed us paper towels, to get us out of there faster.

"Thank you," said Mom. We dried our faces, and Mom put on her Pagoda red Helena Rubenstein lipstick. "How do I look, Justine?"

"Great, Mom." She didn't care if my tone was derisive, as long as I said the right words.

As we left the ladies' room we saw a sign: "Patti Page, appearing nightly on the Starlight Roof."

"Look at that! This is no coincidence. Maybe we were meant to come here today and see Patti Page. Come! I have an idea."

"Mom, you need to get a job. Let's concentrate on that."

"I'm going to buy a new hat, and then we'll go see Patti Page tonight."

"What money do you have?"

"Trust me."

"Trust you? I'll trust you if you act normal." But I didn't know what else to do. We walked over to Alexander's department store on Lexington Avenue and Fifty-Eighth Street. The first floor was a jumble of large steel-rimmed bins filled with hats, purses, and shoes from $2.99 to $10.99. Mom tried on some summery cloth hats with wide brims. (Mom claimed she was the one who got Bella Abzug wearing those hats when they were in Hunter College together.) She found a pale yellow one that highlighted her complexion, and tilting her head to the side, she smiled in the mirror. I tried on a hat too, a white one with a blue ribbon and a medium brim. A middle-aged saleslady with kind eyes watched us as we preened, and I thought,

I don't know where we're sleeping tonight and we have hardly any money but just for this moment, someone admires us.

My mother turned to me. "How do I look?"

"Fine."

"Just fine?"

"You look really pretty."

The saleslady came over and adjusted my hat. I explained to her, "My mother's father used to own a hat store. She loves hats."

"Well, you look lovely too, dear. Even better than your mother."

My mother gave her a sharp look. "Well, you should have seen me at her age."

The lady frowned and didn't know what to say. She walked away, and I took off the hat. As my mother went to the cashier, she muttered under her breath, "Troublemaker."

Mom ripped the tag off and wore the hat out. We stopped at Bickford's for coffee for her, juice for me and we shared an English muffin. Then we walked to Eighth Avenue to the post office in case the check from Dad had come. It was unlikely that it would be there now that she had abducted me, but it was worth a shot. But there was nothing.

We passed an hour at Tad's, where we had a potato and a piece of garlic bread each. Then hung around the library until about seven before returning to the Waldorf.

In the restroom at the Waldorf Mom combed her hair and swept it up a bit, holding it in place with bobby pins. When the attendant wasn't looking, Mom took a flower from the flower arrangement and stuck it in her hair behind her ear. Finally she freshened her lipstick. Radiant again.

We went upstairs to the Starlight, packed with upper-class couples having dinner. Patti Page dazzled in a shiny blue off-the-shoulder dress. Accompanied by a pianist, she sang "A Poor Man's Roses."

When we moved in from the entrance, making our way toward an empty table, the maître d' spoke to us, warily. "Do you have a reservation for dinner?"

"Not exactly. A glass of lemonade for the little girl." She turned away from him and sat down as we watched Patti Page. I watched a lady eat shrimp cocktail out of a silver bowl with a tiny silver fork.

"This is for dinner only—"

"Don't worry about it," Mom told him. "We won't be here that long. Just bring the little girl a lemonade." She nodded at him reassuringly. "It's just for a few minutes."

He frowned but walked away. Patti Page finished the song and people clapped gently. Patti Page started singing "It Had To Be You," one of Mom's favorites, and Mom started murmuring the words.

Some others I've seen, might never be mean
Might never be cross, or try to be boss
But they wouldn't do—

Then Mom started singing. She had a confident voice, but I would have given anything for her to stop singing. People turned around, surprised but not annoyed. Mom stood up as she sang with Page.

For nobody else, gave me a thrill—with all your faults,
I love you still.

Page smiled and nodded, giving her permission to continue. They sang the rest of the song together.

It had to be you, wonderful you
It had to be you.

They sang through the whole song, and people clapped as they finished. The waiter brought me a lemonade and I concentrated on drinking it, looking down as the applause subsided.

"Miss Page, would you let me sing a song that I wrote?" I looked up, *oh no.*

Page hesitated perhaps a fraction of a section. "Go ahead honey. You can sing one song."

Mom looked at me with a glint in her eye. As she walked to the stage I could hardly breathe.

"You said you wrote this song?"

"Yes, Miss Page. I did."

Mom carried herself with poise, back straight, chin up. Page handed the microphone to her and she started singing:

Love is a mutual affair.
A feeling two people may share

The pianist accompanied her a little. Mom smiled at me.

I want you, need you, love you.
But you must want, love and need me too

I dared to look at the audience. They found her endearing. She was a pretty middle-aged woman, taking a moment in the limelight. Maybe they wondered if they could do as well if they had the nerve to sing at the Waldorf.

Tell me what I want to know.
What feelings for you may I show?

It was a short song, and in a few more sentences it would be over. Blissfully Mom didn't drag it out. Page joined her at the end and sang the final words with her.

That only a two-some may share.

Page smiled graciously.

"Thank you," Mom whispered.

"That was sweet, love," Page said.

Mom handed back the microphone and walked back to me. She sat down, on Cloud 9. We stayed there awhile, as she got herself calmed down. I'd saved half the lemonade for her, and she drank it.

"Let's go," she finally said.

When we got outside I felt a surge of relief. That's when she told me the truth. She'd actually been thinking of asking Patti Page to help us. "I'm out of money. I don't know where to turn," she said. She sighed, and I searched her face. Such sadness. My heart was breaking for her. "I wish Grandpa was still alive," she said. "He wouldn't let this happen to me." I thought to myself, "Wouldn't let this happen to *us,* Mom."

We stopped for a light, and she stroked the top of my head. "I'll call the boys," she suggested.

"I don't think you should do that, Mom."

I yearned for my brothers, for that sense of belonging that I only had with them. But I was afraid they would turn us in. I wanted to go back to PCS, but I didn't want to have another scene with the police. "Really, Mom, don't."

We rode the IND train to the end of Brooklyn. Somewhere in Brighton Beach we walked along Ocean Parkway, and stopped in a quiet funeral home to use the ladies' room. It had a chaise lounge, an armchair and we had it to ourselves. Mom got the idea of spending the night there, and that's what we did. She slept in the armchair and I slept on the chaise lounge. We didn't see one person in that funeral home.

The next day Mom again suggested calling the boys. I told her not to, but my words didn't register with her. She found a public phone and called Leo at his apartment on Fifth Street.

"Leo, it's Mom.

"Mom—"

"Meet us at Alexander's in an hour," she ordered.

He knew what he had to do, but it was something he dreaded.

"Okay," he told her.

"We'll be near women's hats on the main floor. Oh, Leo, have you seen the creep?"

"Yeah, we saw Dad."

"Did he give you any money?"

"Yeah, a little."

"Well, bring us whatever you have. We need it."

As Mom and I made our way back to Alexander's, a huge billboard for *The Ten Commandments*, a reissue of the 1950s movie, with Charlton Heston looking strong and righteous as Moses, loomed over us.

The store was more crowded than yesterday, as it was lunchtime now. Mom was trying on hats again when Leo waved from a distance. As he approached us, I saw in Leo's clamped-down expression that he'd called Dad. I kissed him on the cheek.

"How're ya doing, Juz?"

"Don't do anything," I whispered.

Leo looked at me, his eyes direct and appealing to me for forgiveness. "It's out of my hands now," he whispered. I was hyper aware, and looked past him. Outside, behind the glass entrance, was my father with two policemen. There was such a bustle of shoppers, that Mom didn't see them. Mixed with the tension in Leo's eyes was relief now that he'd handed over responsibility. "We were worried about you," he said. "We were afraid you would disappear with her."

"I know, but...."

Mom kissed him. She didn't see my father or the cops, and was oblivious to the fraughtness of the situation.

"Let's go get something to eat," he said.

"Now you're talking." She was delighted by his suggestion, and didn't realize that Leo didn't usually take the lead. He avoided Mom's gaze.

"Come Justine, we'll get some nice soupy."

"There's a coffee shop this way," Leo said as we started to follow him out.

Later Leo told me that when Mom called him, he debated whether or not to call Dad. But it would have been impossible for the boys to stand up to Mom without adult help. I wanted to go back to Pleasantville, to the security of my bed, and meals I could count on, and the comfort of Lillie, and my friends there and the structure of the place.

"Be careful, Mom." I stopped walking but Mom didn't hear me and kept going. Leo stopped in between us, uncertain what to do. Shoppers were all around us. I looked outside and Dad and I exchanged glances.

Leo nudged me. "Come on, Justine."

"I don't want her to be taken away in handcuffs again." I yelled, "Mom! Mom!"

She turned and saw me being firm and that Leo was shaken. Now she knew something was up.

"What's going on?" She followed Leo's gaze outside and saw Dad.

Suddenly she was furious, like a general, and glared at him. "How could you do this to me," she barked.

I put my hand on her arm."He's trying to help, Mom."

She moved toward him. "You traitor!"

Leo was paralyzed, and I gripped her arm harder to stop her from slapping him.

"Let's go, Mom! We've gotta get out of here!" She saw that she still had one devoted trooper—but I saw her as a stranger might see her, wild and cornered.

What I wished had happened next: Leo gently but firmly holds me. Dad comes over and says in a kind way, "Martha, please let us take Justine back to Pleasantville. It's best for her right now." Mom stops resisting and steps back. My father leads me away. The cops drive us to the school. My father hugs and kisses me. "I'm glad you're safe. Maybe we can figure out a way for you to come live with me."

But that's not what happened. Dad gestured to the police and they started coming inside, moving rapidly through the shoppers. "Coming through, coming through here!"

I pushed Mom toward the other side of the store. "Just go, Mom!" We jostled and weaved our way rapidly through the crowd. She followed me, that charged look in her eye. She loved it when her loyal lieutenants took care of her. I was charged up too and kept yelling, "Excuse me! Excuse us! Emergency!" as we elbowed our way out.

The cops and Dad followed. Mom and I reached the exit door and burst out of it. Halfway down the block a taxi stopped with a passenger just getting out. I raced to it.

"Run, Mom!" I got in and a few seconds later she got in, breathless.

"Sixty-Fifth Street and Fifth Avenue, please," I said. I thought I was just ad-libbing, but maybe a part of me wanted to go there.

The taxi started going and the light was with us. I ducked down but after a block I turned around and peered through the back window. Dad and the cops ran out of Alexander's and Leo came through the door behind them. But we were gone.

The taxi stopped in front of Temple Emanuel. Mom had just enough to pay the fare. We stepped out and opened the door of the synagogue as though we had found refuge. We went inside the quiet sanctuary and Mom plopped down on a padded bench in a back pew and sighed heavily. "I need to rest."

The muted, soft lighting was a comfort.

"You are a smart cookie," she said.

"Thanks, Mom."

She closed her eyes. I looked around, feeling the velvet of the cushion, trying to calm down. Now the elderly man who'd confronted me the last time I was there came in fussing with something. He remembered me and stopped.

"Hey, what do you want? What gives here?"

"We have to see the rabbi," I said.

"No, no. I remember you. You have to go."

Nobody was stopping me.

"My mother's not feeling well. We need to see the rabbi."

He tried to ignore me and spoke to Mom.

"You can't just disturb the rabbi, lady. Go home if you're not feeling well."

I stood up. "Mom, I'll go find him."

"Okay, okay," he said. "I'll see if he's free." He moved slowly. He made me sick, this narrow-minded little man. Couldn't he see we needed help? Wasn't a synagogue supposed to be a place that cared for people?

"Look, just get the rabbi, will ya?"

He shook his head and left. Mom leaned back and sighed. "You're a chip off the old block." When circumstances forced me to, I thought. I looked at the huge flower arrangement in front of the *bima,* the platform in front of the arc. It occurred to me to take a flower for Mom. With my luck, the guy would probably catch me and it would be more embarrassment on top of everything. And I hated it when my mother took things like that. But this was a crisis; she needed a flower right now. I got up and walked to the front of the room and took a small rose. I walk back to Mom and broke most of the stem off.

"Here, Mom. For you." I tucked the flower into Mom's hair.

"Oh, that's nice. Do I look all right?"

"Yeah, Mom. You look beautiful."

I sat next to her. "I'm going back to Pleasantville, Mom."

She took a moment to let that sink in.

"After all we've been through together? You wouldn't do that to me."

Guilt stabbed me in the heart. Was this a mistake? No, she shouldn't have put me through this ordeal. "Mom, I'm going to."

"Don't disappoint me, Justine."

"I'm sick of living like this, Mom."

"I'm doing the best I can."

"I know, Mom. But you need help."

"Of course I need help! But the only thing people do is abandon me! Your father abandoned me. Your brothers. And now you."

Tears came to my eyes as I took her hand. "Mom, I'm not abandoning—"

She interrupted me. "Oh yes you are! What, you think you're gonna get in good with your father now? He should drop dead! He and that—that bastard concubine! They ruined my life!"

"But, Mom, it's not my fault!"

"You think I've been a bad mother? There are mothers who beat their children, who let their children live in filth. You're lucky to have me as a mother."

After all she had put me through, I couldn't believe my ears.

"You—you—you're not such a good mother!"

"Who do you think you're talking to? I gave birth to you. I raised you. I nurtured you. I took care of you when you were sick."

"But you *don't* take care of me when I'm sick. You don't do those things any more!"

"So when things get tough, you sell out to the other side."

"Mom, I'm just a kid."

She put on her most authoritative voice. "Show some loyalty. If you love me, you'll stand by me."

"If *you* really loved *me*, you wouldn't want me to suffer just because you're suffering."

Mom was momentarily speechless.

"Mommy, I have to go back. It's the best thing."

She was crying now. "What did I do wrong, Justine, that my children should be taken from me like this?"

I could feel my face crumpling, as I gave in to full crying. "We still have each other, Mom. I still love you."

"Do you, Justine?"

I nodded tearfully and put my arm around her. We leaned our heads together.

"I love you, Justine."

"I love you too, Mom.

Mom pulled out a tissue and wiped her eyes. "Tell me one reason why you love me."

We almost laughed, recognizing that Mom was such an egomaniac. I was willing to indulge her.

"Because you've got style, Mom."

She was smiling as the rabbi came in. "I'm Rabbi Stein. What can I do for you?"

"What can you do for me?" Mom shook her head. "Where do I begin?"

I cut her off. "My mother needs help. And a place to stay."

"Well, I'll be happy to call Jewish Family Services for you."

"Ah, here we go again with the agencies. Listen—first of all, you can give my daughter five dollars. She needs train fare back to Westchester."

The rabbi looked at her. Instinctively he knew it was useless to resist. He reached in his pocket and handed me five dollars.

"Thank you," I said.

I gave her a hug and kiss.

"Watch the street when you cross."

In the midst of all this, it pissed me off that she said that. I had to fend for myself with tough emotionally disturbed girls, and loneliness, and she's making like she's a protective mom with, "Watch the street." But we clasped hands and I started out the door. Just as I got there I turned around.

"Mom!"

She looked at me.

"Leo was only trying to help. He did the right thing. Don't stay angry at him."

She nodded.

Outside I took a deep breath and felt some relief. I walked to Grand Central and got a train to Thornwood. I called the operator on a pay phone and said it was an emergency and she connected me to PCS. A supervisor came to pick me up. I didn't know until I got all the way back to Pleasantville that Mom had left a lipstick mark on my cheek.

When I got back to my cottage, several girls—Rhonda, Crystal, Simcha—came running down the stairs, just as some girls did when I first got there. But this time they were really friendly.

"Justine's back!"

I was sheepish. "Hi."

Lillie happily put her arm around me.

"Where you been, girl?"

"Oh, around."

The girls pulled at me. "C'mon. Tell us what happened." We ran upstairs.

I walked into my room. I opened my locker and my shoebox was in there. I took it out and put it on my bed. The girls came in and sat on the bed, watching me. Crystal came in and watched too.

I opened the shoebox and took out the new loafers. I kicked off my old loafers and put on the new ones. They felt so good. Then I threw the old ones in the trash basket.

Rhonda put out her hand for me to slap her five, and I did— not triumphantly, but rather a gesture between survivors.

She went over to the little record player and put on a forty-five of "Big Girls Don't Cry." She started dancing. I did too, and soon everyone joined in. The other girls were funkier dancers than I was, but I danced happily. It was just what I wanted to be doing.

* * *

Epilogue

"That is part of the beauty of all literature. You discover that your longings are universal longings, that you're not lonely and isolated from anyone. You belong."

          - F. Scott Fitzgerald

This memoir is slightly fictionalized but the essential facts of my childhood – six years of chronic homelessness followed by six years as a ward of the court in placement with the Jewish Child Care Association – are completely true. My mother and I stayed in about 23 hotels and apartments in Manhattan from the time I was five until I was eleven. My brothers were with us for five of those years.

I lived at the Pleasantville Cottage School for three years, and when I was fourteen I moved to a group residence for teenage girls in Rego Park, Queens. During my last year of high school I moved in with my father and stepmother before heading off to college at SUNY Purchase.

I studied literature and went to England for my junior year abroad, followed by a year in France after I graduated. Years later I got a master's degree in screenwriting from Columbia University and did a fellowship year in Los Angeles. I got married and had two beautiful children. I've sold screenplays, written for numerous magazines, newspapers and websites, and have had two books published. For the last 10 years I've worked as a university administrator.

My brothers both became lawyers and have wonderful children.

My mother remarried to a nice man she met at a peace rally. Maintaining a relationship with her was always a struggle, but I did, on a limited basis.

Over the years I became close to my father. He taught me to file my papers, make perfect hard-boiled eggs and to pay my taxes. He gave me driving lessons, insisted I learn to change a tire and helped me get my driver's license. He taught me how to use an electric drill, put up shelves, and repair things around the house. This was how he showed his love.

My parents have passed away. I tried to absorb their best qualities—my father's practicality, my mother's creativity. Both my parents had soulful, visionary moments that remain with me. I tried to convey those qualities to my children as I raised them, and I see those qualities, and more, in them all the time. My children are my life's greatest blessing.

Acknowledgements

Many people helped me get this book written and I gratefully thank all of them.

Special thank you to:

Steve Sander and Betty Marton, for their stalwart friendship, love, soulfulness and support.

Barbara Zucker for her wisdom, warmth and loyalty.

The New York Foundation for the Arts, the Millay Colony for the Arts and the Wallace-Reader's Digest Fund.

The girls and boys I shared my childhood with in the Pleasantville Cottage School; my 6th grade teacher John Palmieri, and to the beloved memories of Tom Crank, Lillian Wright, Betty Taylor and Bruce Quinn.

Alice Schaeffer Nadelman, my kind, dynamic and devoted social worker at PCS, who stayed in touch with me and other girls for years. Some of the dialogue in Chapter 9 comes from her article in *Mutual Aid Groups and the Life Cycle*, F. E. Peacock Publishers, Illinois, 1986, and is used with her permission.

Cheryl Strayed and *The Rumpus* family.

Dan Mausner, archivist extraordinaire, for keeping me organized.

Editors: Dan Mausner, Betty Marton, Elissa Bassist, Asher Klein, Penny Prince, Elly Kalfus and Diane Strack.

For sharing their memories: Jackie Lazarowitz Heagle, Roslyn Eisenstein Castellano, George Wolinsky, David Fischer, Robert Casten, Linda Martin, Valerie Storfer.

The many friends and compatriots in writing workshops.

Creative collaboration: Jeof Vita, Catherine Ritzinger, Barbara Ehlers, Jerry Teters and Jodie Trapani.

For providing tangible and intangible support: Amy Steinberg, Virginia Thomas, Mary Menzel, Donna Henken, Brian Lindstrom, Maureen Ryan, David Hajdu, Ric Burns, Quandra Prettyman, Margaret Lew, Shannon Firth, David Bornstein, Alanna Blau, Yeshvir Daamineni, Meakin Armstrong, Jane Spinak, the late Lewis Cole, Tom March and Richard Kost.

Asher and Grace, for always keeping me inspired.

Please visit justinehopeblau.com